The Merchant of Venice

William Shakespeare

A GCSE revision guide
devised and written by Janet Oliver

The right of Janet Oliver to be identified as Author of this Work has been asserted by her in accordance with the Copyright, Designs and Patents Act 1988

First published 2020

ISBN 978-1-9163827-0-1

© Vega Publishing LTD 2020

Vega Publishing LTD, 12 Glebe Avenue, Woodford Green, Essex IG8 9HB United Kingdom

Design by Martin Cadwallader

Contents

Introduction
How to use this book

'The Merchant of Venice' is one of Shakespeare's most famous plays. The story covers love, hate, revenge, greed and disguise, and has entertained audiences for hundreds of years. Its universal appeal is obvious but tackling such a wide-ranging play in a short exam is a real challenge.

This guide is written and laid out to help you with your revision of 'The Merchant of Venice' and to ensure that your examination response is focused and clear. It is designed to show you how to address the most important elements that the examiner is looking for:

- **Language analysis**
- **Effective use of quotations**
- **Exploration of themes**
- **Understanding of characters**
- **The context of the play**

The book is divided into sections of characters and themes with a box at the top of each section which gives a strong, clear overview of the character or theme.

The section is then dealt with using 5-8 key quotations which are in **bold** font. Literary devices are in ***bold italics.***

The analysis of each quotation relates directly to the theme or character. Some of the points are fairly straightforward and some are much more analytical.

The context is added at the end to show how it can be woven into an answer with a relevant quotation. Context means the social, historical and literary influences of the time that Shakespeare was writing in and how these are reflected in the play.

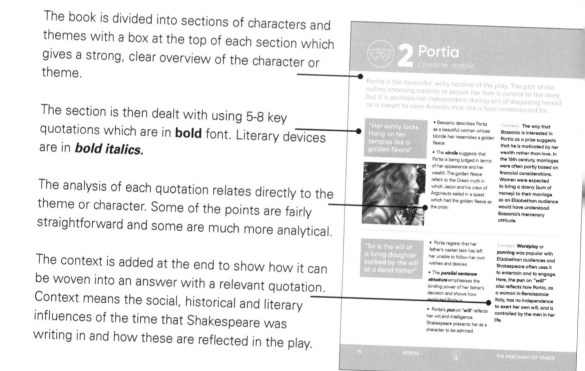

There is also a yellow box entitled 'Grade 9 Exploration' in each chapter. This shows you how you can look at alternative interpretations of the play, which are crucial for gaining a grade of 7 or above.

Look out for the colourful mindmap. It condenses four main points from the chapter, including the Grade 9 Exploration box, into four strands. The information is in a shortened format; if you want to keep your revision really focused, use the mind map to make sure you remember the key features of the chapter.

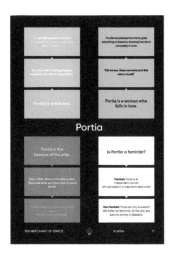

The sample essay follows. This is based on a four paragraph formula which answers the question clearly and analytically. The font is small as there is so much detail but, if you are wondering what a top level answer looks like, do read it carefully.

Below that, there is a box with essential exam tips: lots of good ideas and reminders that will help you on exam day.

At the back of the book, there is a glossary of all the literary terms and a list of the quotations with act and scene references. You really don't need to learn these references; they are only included to help you find the place in the play for your own revision.

Timeline
Plot Summary

Act 1

Bassanio wishes to marry Portia but does not have enough money to court her.

Antonio agrees to lend him the money. His money is tied up with his ships so he tells Bassanio to take out a loan in his name.

Portia is frustrated about the casket test which prevents her from choosing her own husband. The casket test has been set by her dead father and means that she has to marry the man who chooses the correct casket.

Shylock agrees to lend Antonio the money. It is clear that Antonio despises Shylock for his religion and race. In turn, Shylock hates Antonio and uses the loan as a chance to get his revenge for all the humiliation Antonio has piled upon him. Shylock's condition of the loan is that Antonio will need to give a pound of flesh if he is not able to repay the money in time.

Act 2

Shylock's servant, Launcelot, leaves his service to work for Bassanio. He delivers Jessica's letter to her lover, Lorenzo.

Lorenzo and his friends help Jessica to escape from Shylock's house. Armed with money that she has stolen from her father, Jessica leaves to marry Lorenzo.

Two of Portia's suitors try and fail the casket test.

Shylock is devastated by his daughter's betrayal. There are rumours that Antonio's ships have been delayed and that it will be difficult for Antonio to repay his loan on time.

Act 3

News comes to Shylock that Jessica is spending all of his money and that another of Antonio's ships is lost at sea.

Bassanio takes the casket task and passes it, becoming engaged to Portia. At the same time, Gratiano and Nerissa announce their engagement. Both couples swear their love through the exchange of rings.

News arrives of Antonio's troubles and Bassanio and Gratiano sail to Venice to help him. Portia and Nerissa disguise themselves as men and secretly follow them.

Antonio asks Shylock for mercy but Shylock is determined to have his bond.

Act 4

As he cannot repay the loan, Antonio is brought to court and Shylock demands the payment of the pound of flesh, ignoring all pleas for mercy.

Portia arrives, dressed as a male lawyer. She saves Antonio by arguing that Shylock cannot take the flesh without spilling Christian blood, which is illegal.

Shylock is punished for plotting to kill Antonio by paying a hefty fine and becoming a Christian.

Portia and Nerissa are still dressed as men. They ask for the rings from their husbands as rewards for saving Antonio. Reluctantly, both men give their rings away.

Act 5

The action moves back to Belmont where Lorenzo and Jessica await Portia's return.

Portia and Nerissa pretend to be outraged by their husbands giving their rings away. Then they reveal the truth: that they were the lawyer and the assistant. Antonio is told that his ships are safe. The play ends on a note of harmony.

1 Antonio
Character analysis

Antonio is the Venetian merchant who values his friendship with Bassanio so highly that he agrees to an unusual grisly loan from Shylock. In the dramatic climax of the courtroom scene, he comes close to dying but in the end is saved.

"In sooth, I know not why I am so sad"

- Antonio is unsure why he feels unhappy.

- These are the opening words of the play and are used to establish a character who is dejected and sorrowful.

- No reason is given for his sadness and this sense of mystery intrigues the audience.

Context: 'A Merchant of Venice' is a comedy yet the opening words set a melancholy (sad) tone for the play. Shakespeare often merged comic and tragic elements together in his plays to enhance the comedy, engage the audience and explore human nature; another of his comedies, 'Twelfth Night' also opens with one of the characters, Orsino, in an unhappy emotional state.

"I think he only loves the world for him"

- Salarino says that Antonio has an incredibly deep love for Bassanio.

- The men's friendship is clearly an intense one. The **adverb 'only'** shows the exclusivity and depth of Antonio's love.

Context: An audience might wonder whether this friendship has its basis in homosexual love yet male friendships in Elizabethan society were often emotionally intense.

> **"All my fortunes are at sea"**
> **"Dangerous rocks... enrobe the roaring waters with my silks"**

- Antonio admits that he has no spare money as he waits for his merchant ships to return to Venice. There are plenty of references in the play to the perils of sea journeys.

- The metaphor highlights the treacherous nature of the boats' journeys. The **adjectives** **'dangerous'** and **'roaring'** emphasise the vicious nature of the sea which can easily destroy the fragile boats and their cargo.

- Antonio is a businessman, the eponymous Merchant of Venice, yet an audience might question Antonio's business sense as he states that **'all'** his fortunes are at risk at one time.

Context: Venice was one of the great trading ports of Europe and Shakespeare's audience was aware of its reputation as a place where enormous wealth was generated. Yet they were also aware of the perilous nature of sea journeys and so a sense of unease is created as Antonio later pledges to return money which he does not yet have and is reliant on the uncertain nature of trading at sea.

> **"How true a gentleman"**

- Lorenzo speaks highly of Antonio.

- In a play where the lie between appearance and reality are often blurred, Lorenzo is earnest and sincere in his praise of Antonio as a **'true'** or genuine man of honour.

- He directs the audience's response so that we admire Antonio and are anxious about his fate.

> "The weakest kind of fruit drops earliest to the ground"

- Antonio accepts his death, saying that he is weak and so will die young.

- He sees himself as flawed and weak. This perhaps links to the opening of the play, where he is melancholy and depressed without any good reason.

- His view of himself is arguably a result of his knowledge that the situation is his own fault and so he deserves to die. He was foolish to sign the grisly bond with Shylock and arrogant in assuming that his ships would return in time.

Grade 9 Exploration:
Look at the character in a different way

How sympathetic is Antonio as a character?

Sympathetic: The drama of the courtroom scene as Antonio is taken to the brink of death directs the audience's response to feel great pity for Antonio. He accepts his death without grovelling for mercy, understanding that **'the duke cannot deny the course of the law'**. He knows that the law has to be upheld and there is a nobility in the way he accepts this, even as the audience watches the grisly visual spectacle of Shylock **'earnestly'** sharpening his knife. This is horrifying and our sympathy is with Antonio. Later, despite being saved, Antonio does not find happiness with a loved one by the last scene. He contrasts with the happy couples in Act 5 and ends the play as he began: isolated and melancholy.

Unsympathetic: Antonio is not an admirable character. His bigoted treatment of Shylock is appalling, dehumanising him by calling him a **'cut-throat dog'**. Antonio has also physically abused Shylock by spitting on his cloak which shows complete contempt. This lack of religious tolerance would have been commonplace in Elizabethan England but modern, post-Holocaust audiences who watch the play often find it difficult to sympathise with the prejudiced Antonio.

Essential Exam Tip

☑ Read the play on your own at home. Try listening to an audio book as well.

☑ Refer to different places within the play. Don't just write about the start of the play, for example, as that doesn't show the examiner that you have a good understanding of the whole play.

The men's friendship is clearly an intense one. The **adverb** 'only' shows the exclusivity and depth of Antonio's love.

An audience might question Antonio's business sense as he states that **'all'** his fortunes are at risk at one time.

'I think he only loves the world for him'

'All my fortunes are at sea'

Antonio is a great friend to Bassanio.

Antonio is a businessman.

Antonio

Antonio is a character who suffers.

Do we sympathise with Antonio?

'The weakest kind of fruit drops earliest to the ground'

Yes: The drama of the courtroom with Shylock sharpening his knife directs the audience's response to feel great pity for Antonio.

Antonio sees himself as failing and weak in the courtroom scene, knowing that he has been foolish.

No: Modern audiences in particular find it hard to sympathise with Antonio who mistreats Shylock in such an appalling way.

Sample GCSE Exam Question

Read the following extract from Act 4 Scene 1.
Answer both questions below the text.

At this point in the story, Antonio is waiting for Shylock to take the pound of flesh.

ANTONIO

But little: I am arm'd and well prepared.
Give me your hand, Bassanio: fare you well!
Grieve not that I am fallen to this for you;
For herein Fortune shows herself more kind
Than is her custom: it is still her use
To let the wretched man outlive his wealth,
To view with hollow eye and wrinkled brow
An age of poverty; from which lingering penance
Of such misery doth she cut me off.

Commend me to your honourable wife:
Tell her the process of Antonio's end;
Say how I loved you, speak me fair in death;
And, when the tale is told, bid her be judge
Whether Bassanio had not once a love.
Repent but you that you shall lose your friend,
And he repents not that he pays your debt;
For if the Jew do cut but deep enough,
I'll pay it presently with all my heart.

a) Discuss how Antonio is presented in the extract.
b) Discuss how Antonio is presented in the play as a whole.

 # Sample GCSE Answer

 Start with the point that Antonio seems to have accepted his fate

In the extract, Antonio is at the brink of death but seems to be resigned to his fate, saying **'I am arm'd and well prepared'**. The ***declarative sentence*** shows a confidence as he gets ready to die, an acceptance of his fate. This strength and confidence is emphasised through the forceful pattern of imperative ***verbs*** to start his sentences in this speech: **'give' 'fare' 'grieve'.** The impact which this gives his sentences reminds us that Antonio is a man of courage and honour who meets his fate with clarity and purpose, ensuring that the audience empathises with him and sees him as a man of nobility. This nobility is reinforced later in the extract as he asks Bassanio to **'commend me to your honourable wife'**; Antonio's language is dignified and selfless even as he sees Shylock's knife being sharpened before him; he does not grovel and beg for mercy but retains control of himself. There is perhaps an air of the tragic hero about him here with his reference to himself in the third person; he says **'tell her the process of Antonio's end'**. By replacing 'my' with **'Antonio',** he seems to elevate himself to almost hero status. Alternatively, the use of the third person could be a sudden, desperate attempt to deny the reality of his imminent death, to cowardly pretend that it is happening to someone else. Yet elsewhere in the play, the characters speak highly and so again direct the audience's response. Lorenzo says of him **'how true a gentleman'** and, in a play where the lines between appearance and reality are often blurred, Lorenzo is earnest and sincere in his praise of Antonio as a **'true'** or genuine man of honour.

 Move to the point that Antonio is a businessman

Antonio is not just a gentleman; he is also a merchant, a man of commerce. It could be that he accepts his death as he knows that he is financially ruined and so has lost his position as a respected merchant of Venice. He speaks of fortune which allows **'the wretched man outlive his wealth,/To view with hollow eye and wrinkled brow/An age of poverty'**. A negative image of an old age spent in poverty is created through the use of the *adjectives* 'wretched', 'hollow', 'wrinkle'; it would seem that Antonio values his wealth so much that he is happy to die rather than grow old without it. He certainly does not beg for mercy, and part of the reason is that he understands that **'the duke cannot deny the course of the law'**; he knows that Shylock is entitled to his gruesome bond by law and no one, not even the duke, can stop him. Venice was one of the great trading ports of Europe and its laws protected the trade and wealth that its citizens enjoyed. The duke is unable to override this law to help Antonio in case it undermined the trading that is vital to Venice's prosperity and Antonio, the experienced businessman, understands this. His acceptance of the situation is reflected in the certainty of the *modal verb* 'cannot' which highlights how all have no choice but to obey the laws of Venice.

☑ Explore whether Antonio is, perhaps, defined by his relationship with Bassanio

Despite his life dealing with trade and commerce, Antonio is a man who feels strong emotions. The play opens with a demonstration of how much Antonio loves his friend Bassanio as he offers everything to help Bassanio win Portia. This great friendship is clearly evident in the extract, as it is to Bassanio that Antonio turns to in what he believes are his final minutes with the command **'give me your hand'**. The audience witnesses Antonio's emotional outpouring as he tells Bassanio to **'say how I loved you'**. The men's friendship is clearly an intense one and we see this elsewhere in the play when Salarino states that Antonio has an incredibly deep love for Bassanio: **'I think he only loves the world for him'**. The *adverb* 'only' shows the exclusivity of this friendship, and the audience sees the depth of the emotion that Antonio feels. An audience might wonder whether this friendship has its basis in homosexual love yet male friendships in Elizabethan society were often emotionally intense.

☑ Move to the point that Antonio is drawn into folly through his friendship

This deep friendship draws Antonio into mortal danger. In the extract, he tells Bassanio to **'grieve not that I am fallen to this for you'**, acknowledging that it was his friendship that led him to this point of death. At the beginning, he admits to Bassanio that he has no spare money to lend him as he waits for his merchant ships to return to Venice, saying **'all my fortunes are at sea'**. Shakespeare's audience was aware of Venice's reputation as a place where enormous wealth was generated yet they were also aware of the perilous nature of sea journeys, and so a sense of unease is created as Antonio pledges to return money which he does not yet have. He seems foolhardy in doing so, and this sense of unease is increased with frequent references in the play to the perils of sea journeys such as **'dangerous rocks'** and **'enrobe the roaring waters with my silks'**. The *metaphor* highlights the treacherous nature of the boats' journeys and the *adjectives* 'dangerous' and 'roaring' emphasise the vicious nature of the sea which can easily destroy the fragile boats and their cargo. Antonio's confidence in borrowing money from Shylock against such dangerous ventures seems misplaced and so the audience doubts his wisdom.

☑ Explore how much sympathy the audience feels for Antonio

Yet despite the self-induced folly which leads to Antonio accepting Shylock's terms, the drama of the courtroom scene as Antonio is taken to the brink of death directs the audience's response to feel great pity for Antonio. The grisly visual spectacle of Shylock **'earnestly'** sharpening his knife is horrifying and we see Antonio humbled as he sees himself as flawed, stating that **'the weakest kind of fruit drops earliest to the ground'**. Antonio accepts his death, saying that he is fragile and so will die young. And, despite being saved, Antonio does not find happiness with a loved one. He *contrasts* with the happy couples in Act 5 and ends the play as he began: isolated and melancholy. Yet audiences might not have so much sympathy with him as they consider his bigoted treatment of Shylock. Antonio calls Shylock **'cut-throat dog'** and, by reducing Shylock to the status of an animal, the audience is aware that Shylock is dehumanised. Antonio has also physically abused Shylock by spitting on his cloak which shows his complete contempt. Christianity was a cornerstone of society in Elizabethan England and Antonio's lack of religious tolerance would not be as shocking for Shakespeare's audience as it is for a modern audience. Indeed, modern audiences who watch the play post-Holocaust often find it difficult to sympathise with Antonio. Like many of Shakespeare's characters, our response to him is complicated and determined by the direction of the production.

Portia is the beautiful, witty heroine of the play. The plot of the suitors choosing caskets to secure her love is central to the story, but it is perhaps her independent daring act of disguising herself as a lawyer to save Antonio that she is best remembered for.

"Her sunny locks/ Hang on her temples like a golden fleece"

- Bassanio describes Portia as a beautiful woman whose blonde hair resembles a golden fleece.

- The **simile** suggests that Portia is being judged in terms of her appearance and her wealth. The golden fleece refers to the Greek myth in which Jason and his crew of Argonauts sailed in a quest which had the golden fleece as the prize.

Context: The way that Bassanio is interested in Portia as a prize suggests that he is motivated by her wealth rather than love. In the 16th century, marriages were often partly based on financial considerations. Women were expected to bring a dowry (sum of money) to their marriage so an Elizabethan audience would have understood Bassanio's mercenary attitude.

"So is the will of a living daughter curbed by the will of a dead father"

- Portia regrets that her father's casket task has left her unable to follow her own wishes and desires.

- The **parallel sentence structure** emphasises the binding power of her father's decision and shows how restricted Portia is.

- Portia's **pun** on 'will' reflects her wit and intelligence. Shakespeare presents her as a character to be admired.

Context: Wordplay or **punning** was popular with Elizabethan audiences and Shakespeare often uses it to entertain and to engage. Here, the **pun** on *"will"* also reflects how Portia, as a woman in Renaissance Italy, has no independence to exert her own will, and is controlled by the men in her life.

"This house, these servants and this same myself"

- Portia gives herself entirely to Bassanio when they become betrothed.

- The *list* emphasises that she is giving everything; interestingly, she places herself as the last item in the *list*, possibly implying that the material possessions are of more interest to him.

Context: In the 16th century, women were the property of their husbands. They had no legal rights and could not own property; Portia's words may seem generous and selfless yet they also reflect the stark reality of the situation as she, and all of her property and wealth, does indeed belong to Bassanio.

"Tarry a little; there is something else. This bond doth give thee here no jot of blood"

- In the courtroom, Portia, masquerading as lawyer, uses the law to save Antonio from his grisly death. It is Portia, a woman, who is the hero of the play. Her intelligence and quick-thinking stops Shylock from collecting the bond and killing Antonio. She is fully in control of the situation.

- The forceful *imperative verb* **'tarry'** (wait) shows that it is Portia in control in the courtroom, giving commands that the men have to abide by. The semi-colon creates a suspenseful pause after **'Tarry a little'**. Portia holds everyone's attention with her enigmatic **'there is something else'**, withholding the information and choosing when to deliver her stunning understanding of the law that will halt Shylock and save Antonio.

> ### "The Jew shall have all justice"

- Portia traps Shylock in the courtroom.

- Despite her words about the importance of mercy at the start of the courtroom scene, she shows none to Shylock. She is cold and meticulous as she ruthlessly traps Shylock in the web of the law.

- She consistently dismissively refers to Shylock as '**the Jew**' or '**Jew**', revealing her entrenched prejudice against him.

Grade 9 Exploration:
Look at the character in a different way

Is Portia a powerful woman?

Yes: Portia runs her household and manages her wealth independently, and Shakespeare presents her as much more sensible and resourceful than her male partner. While Bassanio sighs over Antonio's fate with empty promises, Portia takes control of the situation, moving into a man's world to skilfully manipulate the male-dominated courtroom. She only agrees to marry Bassanio after she has negotiated a position of power by giving the ring that binds Bassanio with conditions to love and respect her.

No: Despite the audience's rapport with Portia, she is not a powerful figure. Any power that Portia does wield in the courtroom scene is because the other characters believe her to be a man; without her male disguise, she would be instantly silenced. She can only succeed in the male world if she denies or hides her femininity. Furthermore, she is ultimately subservient to her husband as the ring is an Elizabethan symbol of female submission. Although she is a character whom we admire, we see her as restricted within a patriarchal (male-dominated) society.

✍ Essential Exam Tips

☑ Make at least three different points about the character/theme based on the extract.

☑ Try to weave points about context into your answer when you are writing about a character or theme. Try not to just bolt the context on at the end or add it in a completely separate paragraph.

The *parallel sentence structure* emphasises the binding power of her father's decision.

The list emphasises how Portia gives everything to Bassanio, showing how she is completely in love.

'So is the will of a living daughter curbed by the will of a dead father'

'this house, these servants and this same myself'

Portia is restricted.

Portia is a woman who falls in love.

Portia

Portia is the heroine of the play.

Is Portia a powerful woman?

'Tarry a little; there is something else./ This bond doth give thee here no jot of blood'

Yes: Portia is an independent woman who succeeds in a male-dominated world.

Portia's intelligence and quick thinking saves Antonio from a grisly death.

No: Portia can only succeed if she hides her femininity. At the end, she submits entirely to Bassanio.

Sample GCSE Exam Question

Read the following extract from Act 3 scene 2.
Answer both questions below the text.
At this point in the play, Portia is waiting for Bassanio to take the casket test.

PORTIA
I pray you, tarry: pause a day or two
Before you hazard; for, in choosing wrong,
I lose your company: therefore forbear awhile.
There's something tells me, but it is not love,
I would not lose you; and you know yourself,
Hate counsels not in such a quality.
But lest you should not understand me well,–
And yet a maiden hath no tongue but thought,–
I would detain you here some month or two
Before you venture for me. I could teach you
How to choose right, but I am then forsworn;

So will I never be: so may you miss me;
But if you do, you'll make me wish a sin,
That I had been forsworn. Beshrew your eyes,
They have o'erlook'd me and divided me;
One half of me is yours, the other half yours,
Mine own, I would say; but if mine, then yours,
And so all yours. O, these naughty times
Put bars between the owners and their rights!
And so, though yours, not yours. Prove it so,
Let fortune go to hell for it, not I.
I speak too long; but 'tis to peize the time,
To eke it and to draw it out in length.

a) How is Portia portrayed in this extract?
b) How is Portia portrayed in the play as a whole?

 # Sample GCSE Answer

 Start with the point that Portia is a woman in love

In the extract, Portia is clearly agitated as she asks Bassanio to delay taking the test; she urges him to **'pause a day or two… forbear awhile'** as she considers the consequences of the test. Her speech veers from one thought to another, showing her unsettled state of mind with the shifts marked by the **conjunctions** **'therefore', 'but', 'and' 'yet'**. These **conjuctions** reflect her confusion and indecision, and sharply **contrast** with her earlier confidence as the lady of Belmont who graciously greets suitors from all over the world. This confidence is undermined when she meets Bassanio as her agitation is rooted in her obvious attraction and love for the dashing young Venetian. At the beginning, she humorously mocked her suitors who did not interest her in the slightest; the opposite is true in this extract as she says to Bassanio **'beshrew your eyes/They have o'erlooked me and divided me'**. The curse of **'beshrew me'** is playful but nevertheless shows how deeply she has been affected by her feelings for Bassanio; the **metaphor** of how his eyes have **'divided'** her shows how love has altered her, creating a whole raft of feelings. Throughout the play, love is seen as a powerful force that motivates the characters and here we see Portia changed through her passionate feelings. Indeed, her love is so strong that she later in the scene gives herself entirely to Bassanio, saying as they are betrothed, **'this house, these servants and this same myself/Are yours, my lord: I give them with this ring'**. The **list** emphasises that she is giving everything; interestingly, she places herself as the last item in the **list**, implying that the material possessions are of more interest. In the 16th century, women were the property of their husbands. They had no legal rights and could not own property; Portia's words may seem generous and selfless yet they also reflect the stark reality of the situation as she, and and all of her property and wealth, does indeed now belong to Bassanio.

Yet despite her overwhelming love for Bassanio and her position as a woman in Renaissance Italy, Portia retains her strength and independence. She openly speaks her mind, even though in the extract she states that **'a maiden hath no tongue but thought'**. Women were supposed to be demure and silent but Portia's long speech is warm, passionate and honest. Indeed, arguably Portia is a model of a feminist character as it is Portia, a woman, who is the hero of the play. Women were not allowed to practise law in Venice and Portia has to disguise herself as a man in order to help Antonio, showing her resourcefulness. Her intelligence and quick thinking stops Shylock from collecting the bond and killing Antonio; just as Shylock prepares to cut and the Christian men helplessly watch, it is the female Portia who controls every aspect of the scene, saying '**tarry a little; there is something else./This bond doth give thee here no jot of blood'**. The forceful *imperative verb* **'tarry'** (wait) establishes that it is Portia in charge in the courtroom, giving commands that the men have to abide by. This power is maintained as her measured sentence structure with its semi-colon creates a suspenseful pause after **'tarry a little'** which ensures that Shylock pauses and the moment of cutting is postponed. With all eyes on her in this tense, dramatic scene, Portia holds their attention with her enigmatic **'there is something else'**, witholding the information and choosing when to deliver her stunning understanding of the law that will halt Shylock and save Antonio. An audience watching this scene is left in little doubt as to who is complete control of the situation: the intelligent Portia. This intelligence is evident the first time that the audience meets her in Act 1; Portia regrets that her father's casket task has left her unable to follow her own desires, and frets that **'so is the will of a living daughter curbed by the will of a dead father'**. The *pun* on **'will'** reflects her wit and intelligence and Shakespeare clearly presents her as a character to be liked and admired.

Yet despite the audience's rapport with Portia, she is not really a powerful figure. Her words about the casket task reflect this as the *parallel sentence structure* emphasises the binding power of her father's decision and shows how restricted Portia is. The **'living daughter'** is controlled by the **'dead father'**, reflecting how even when they have left the world, men control the decisions and desires of the living women. Any power Portia that does wield in the courtroom scene is because the other characters believe her to be a man; without her male disguise, she would be instantly silenced. She can only succeed in the male world if she denies or hides her femininity. Furthermore, she is ultimately subservient to her husband. In the extract, she tells Bassanio that **'one half of me is yours, the other half yours... so all yours'**. The *repetition* of the *pronoun* **'yours'** reinforces this sense of possession as does the ring that she gives Bassanio which is an Elizabethan symbol of female submission. Although she is a character who we admire, we see her as restricted within a patriarchal society.

This portrayal of Portia as a likeable and sympathetic character is evident in the extract. Despite the strength of her feelings for Bassanio, Portia refuses to help him cheat in the test as **'I am then forsworn;/So will I never be'**. She resists temptation, the *modal verb* **'will'** working with the emphatic word **'never'** to reflect how she stops herself from helping Bassanio in the casket test. She shows herself to be a woman of honour and so the audience warms to her. Yet Portia is not wholly good. In the courtroom scene, she is cold and meticulous as she ruthlessly traps Shylock in the web of the law, announcing that **'the Jew shall have all justice'**. Despite her words of mercy at the start of the courtroom scene, she shows none to Shylock and she consistently dismissively refers to Shylock as **'the Jew'** or '**Jew'**, showing her prejudice against him. Portia is a deservedly popular and memorable heroine but audiences note that she is not without flaws.

3 Bassanio
Character analysis

Bassanio is the charming, spendthrift young Venetian man who is beloved of both Antonio and Portia.

"Her sunny locks /Hang on her temples like a golden fleece"

• Bassanio describes Portia as a beautiful woman whose blonde hair resembles a golden fleece.

• The *simile* shows that Bassanio is an ambitious man, interested in Portia for her appearance and her wealth.

• He has been careless with money and now seeks a wife who can improve his fortunes.

Context: The way that Bassanio is interested in Portia as a prize suggests that he is motivated by her wealth rather than love. In the 16th century, marriages were often partly based on financial considerations. Women were expected to bring a dowry (sum of money) to their marriage so an Elizabethan audience would have understood Bassanio's mercenary attitude.

"You shall not seal to such a bond for me: I'll rather dwell in my necessity."

• Bassanio initially refuses to allow Antonio to accept Shylock's terms of the loan.

• Bassanio seems to value his friendship and does not want to place Antonio in any danger.

• Yet, very quickly, Antonio does seal the bond and Bassanio does not really protest again. It would seem that Bassanio is willing to let Antonio risk everything to help him acquire the wealth that he seeks. The audience might well question whether this relationship is an equal one and whether Bassanio is manipulating the friendship to suit his own ends.

"Thou gaudy gold, Hard food for Midas, I will none of thee"

- Bassanio rejects the gold casket.

- He understands that gold can dazzle and blind. The hard **alliteration** of **'gaudy gold'** shows his contempt for the showy, flashy metal. He chooses the lead casket instead, understanding that appearances can be deceptive.

- The audience sees Bassanio as a worthy suitor for Portia. As the winner of the task, he is Portia's true love.

Context: **Bassanio's classical reference to the Greek myth of King Midas, whose touch turned everything to gold, reminds the audience that he is an educated man from a high-born family.**

"Confirm'd, sign'd, ratified by you"

- Bassanio tells Portia that their betrothal must be approved of by her.

- Bassanio is changing from the over-confident youth of Act 1. Porta's goodness and love alters him so that here he shows her the respect and honour due to her.

> "The Jew shall have my flesh, blood, bones and all/Ere thou shalt lose for me one drop of blood"

• Bassanio offers to sacrifice himself for Antonio.

• Bassanio's anguish is evident in the **list** which shows how he is willing to undergo a painful, gruesome death to save his friend. The dreadful situation forces Bassanio to take responsibility for his actions; again, we see that he has changed from the beginning of the play where he casually manipulated his friend.

Context: An audience might wonder whether Antonio and Bassanio's deep friendship has its basis in homosexual love yet male friendships in Elizabethan society were often emotionally intense.

Grade 9 Exploration:
Look at the character in a different way

Is Bassanio a changed character by the end of the play?

Yes: Bassanio begins the play an ambitious, spendthrift young man but learns lessons about love and friendship which change him for the better. An example of this is when he fully admits to Portia in Act 3 that he was a show-off who presented a facade of wealth to impress her. At the end, he tells the truth about giving away the ring, confirming that he is now a man of integrity and honesty, and is worthy of Portia.

No: Bassanio's anguished words in the courtroom offering to put himself in Antonio's place are perhaps empty ones; he knows that the law will not allow this so offers to sacrifice himself, safe in the knowledge it won't be permitted. Even at this moment of high drama, he is full of empty promises and flimsy facades. Furthermore, the audience sees how Bassanio gives the precious ring away under very little pressure from Antonio, and we wonder just how deep and committed his love is. Indeed, when he admits giving away the ring, he says **'If I could add a lie unto a fault,/I would deny it'**. He is still capable of lying if he thinks he can get away with it and is still an ambitious, untrustworthy **'braggart'**.

Essential Exam Tip

☑ Learn quotations off by heart. Write them out on sticky labels and put them in places where you go to all of the time e.g. the kettle or on the bathroom mirror.

The *simile* establishes that Bassanio is interested in Portia for her appearance and wealth.

Bassanio sees through the traps set for him; the hard *alliteration* of 'gaudy gold' reveals his contempt for the showy metal and instead he chooses the lead, understanding that appearances can be deceptive.

'her sunny locks/
Hang on her temples like a golden fleece'

'thou gaudy gold, /
Hard food for Midas, I will none of thee'

Bassanio is a man of ambition.

Bassanio chooses the right casket and wins Portia.

Bassanio

Bassanio learns lessons and becomes a better friend.

Is Bassanio a changed character by the end of the play?

'The Jew shall have my flesh, blood, bones and all/
Ere thou shalt lose for me one drop of blood'

Yes: Bassanio begins the play an ambitious, spendthrift young man but learns lessons about love and friendship which change him for the better.

Bassanio's anguish is evident in the *list* which shows how he is willing to sacrifice himself for his friend.

No: Despite his vows, Bassanio gives his ring away under very little pressure, and we wonder how committed his love for Portia really is.

Read the following extract from Act 1 Scene 1.
Answer both questions below the text.

At this point in the play, Bassanio is persuading Antonio to loan him money so that he can court Portia

BASSANIO
In my school-days, when I had lost one shaft,
I shot his fellow of the self-same flight
The self-same way with more advised watch,
To find the other forth, and by adventuring both
I oft found both: I urge this childhood proof,
Because what follows is pure innocence.
I owe you much, and, like a wilful youth,
That which I owe is lost; but if you please
To shoot another arrow that self way
Which you did shoot the first, I do not doubt,
As I will watch the aim, or to find both
Or bring your latter hazard back again
And thankfully rest debtor for the first.
ANTONIO
You know me well, and herein spend but time
To wind about my love with circumstance;
And out of doubt you do me now more wrong
In making question of my uttermost
Than if you had made waste of all I have:

Then do but say to me what I should do
That in your knowledge may by me be done,
And I am prest unto it: therefore, speak.
BASSANIO
In Belmont is a lady richly left;
And she is fair, and, fairer than that word,
Of wondrous virtues: sometimes from her eyes
I did receive fair speechless messages:
Her name is Portia, nothing undervalued
To Cato's daughter, Brutus' Portia:
Nor is the wide world ignorant of her worth,
For the four winds blow in from every coast
Renowned suitors, and her sunny locks
Hang on her temples like a golden fleece;
Which makes her seat of Belmont Colchos' strand,
And many Jasons come in quest of her.
O my Antonio, had I but the means
To hold a rival place with one of them,
I have a mind presages me such thrift,
That I should questionless be fortunate!

a) Discuss how Bassanio is presented in this extract.

b) Discuss how Bassanio is presented in the play as a whole.

Sample GCSE Answer

☑ **Start with the point that Antonio seems to have accepted his fate**

In the extract, Bassanio is presented as a charming, impetuous man who inspires friendship. He starts to make his request and Antonio tells him to **'but say to me what I should do… and I am prest unto it'**, showing that he is willing to do anything that Bassanio needs or wants. There is great affection between the two and Bassanio reveals this affection in the phrase **'o my Antonio'**; the ***possessive pronoun*** **'my'** captures the closeness between the two men. An audience might wonder whether Antonio and Bassanio's friendship has its basis in homosexual love yet male friendships in Elizabethan society were often emotionally intense.

☑ **Explore whether Bassanio is a man who manipulates**

Bassanio is, arguably, a man who manipulates people and situations. Here in the extract, we see him charm Antonio into lending him money in what could be seen as an exceptionally calculated way. Bassanio starts with a disingenuous honesty, admitting to Antonio that **'I owe you much'**. This seemingly honest ***declarative statement*** is, however, quickly added on to before Antonio can dwell on this fact. Bassanio develops his persuasive speech with the polite, gracious phrase **'but if you please'**, the use of the **conditional tense** suggesting a tentative and diffident approach so that Antonio feels that he is in control even as his friend manipulates him. Bassanio uses the humorous **extended metaphor** of the arrow to convince his friend that this time Antonio's money will be repaid, ending with the confident **declarative statement 'I do not doubt'** to finish, convincing Antonio and leaving no room for concerns. The **structure** of this slick, eloquent speech seems to suggest that Bassanio is extremely manipulative. Later, the audience watches Bassanio initially refusing to allow Antonio to accept Shylock's terms of the loan, declaring **'you shall not seal to such a bond for me: I'll rather dwell in my necessity.'** He seems to value his friendship and does not want to place Antonio in any danger. Yet, very quickly, Antonio does seal the bond and Bassanio does not really protest again. It would seem that Bassanio is willing to let Antonio risk everything to help him acquire the wealth he seeks. The audience might well question whether this relationship is an equal one and whether Bassanio is manipulating the friendship to suit his own ends.

☑ Move to the point that Bassanio is a man of ambition

Certainly, Bassanio has a reason to manipulate the friendship and secure a loan from Antonio. Bassanio is an ambitious young man, clearly stating his aim which is to woo and win Portia who he describes primarily as a **'lady richly left'**. He sees her in terms of her financial status, which, considering what the audience has just learn about his carelessness with money, is an important part of her appeal. He also describes Portia as a beautiful woman whose **'sunny locks/ Hang on her temples like a golden fleece'**. The **simile** shows that Bassanio is a man with aspirations, interested in Portia for her appearance and her wealth. The golden fleece refers to the Greek myth in which Jason and his crew of Argonauts sailed in a quest which had the golden fleece as the prize. In the 16th century, marriages were often based at least in part on financial considerations. Women were expected to bring a dowry (sum of money) to their marriage. The way that Bassanio is interested in Portia as a prize suggests that he is motivated by her wealth rather than love, seeing her money as a way of improving his own lifestyle.

☑ Explore whether Bassanio changes throughout the play

This extract is from the very beginning of the play where Bassanio is careless and ambitious but throughout the play he learns lessons about love and friendship which change him for the better. An example of this is when he tells Portia that their betrothal must be approved of by her: **'confirm'd, sign'd, ratified by you'**. Here, Bassanio is changing from the over-confident youth of Act 1. Porta's goodness and love alters him so that here he shows her the respect and honour due to her and later he fully admits to Portia that **'you shall see how much I was a braggart'**. He freely tells her that he was a show-off who presented a facade of wealth to impress her. At the end, he tells the truth about giving away the ring, revealing that he is now a man of integrity and honesty, and is worthy of Portia. The audience sees how much he has changed from the brash man who spoke greedily about **'a lady richly left'** at the start.

☑ Continue to explore whether Bassanio changes throughout the play

Yet an audience might well question just how far Bassanio is a changed man by the end of the play. Bassanio's anguished words in the courtroom offering to put himself in Antonio's place are perhaps empty ones; he knows that the law will not allow this so offers to sacrifice himself safe in the knowledge that it won't be permitted. Even at this moment of high drama, he is full of empty promises and flimsy facades. Earlier in the play, we wonder whether the reason why Bassanio has managed to open the casket is because he sees through the trap that Portia's father has set. Being a deceiver himself, he is able to see others' attempts to manipulate. He knows that gold can dazzle and blind, saying **'thou gaudy gold/Hard food for Midas, I will none of thee'**. His classical reference to the Greek myth of King Midas, whose touch turned everything to gold, reminds the audience that he is an educated man from a high-born family. The hard **alliteration** of **'gaudy gold'** shows his contempt for the showy, flashy metal and he chooses the lead casket instead, understanding that appearances can be deceptive yet the reason he understands this is because he is adept (skilled) at portraying a false image of himself. Later, the audience sees how Bassanio gives the precious ring away under very little pressure from Antonio, and we wonder just how deep and committed his love for Portia really is. Certainly, we are not entirely sure that he is worthy of the clever, loyal Portia.

4 Shylock
Character analysis

Shylock is the clever businessman who lends money to Antonio and demands a 'pound of flesh' when it cannot be repaid. By the end of the play, he has lost everything: his family, his wealth and even his religion.

"Three thousand ducats; well"

- Shylock muses on the amount of money that Antonio wishes to borrow.

- These are Shylock's first words of the play. Immediately, we associate Shylock with money and business.

- The way he **repeats** the sum creates a sense of greed around Shylock and the **interjection 'well'** suggests that he is musing on the prospect of making more money.

Context: Shakespeare's audience would not have been familiar with Jews as Jews had been expelled from England in 1290. However, Christopher Marlowe's play, 'The Jew of Malta', performed in 1592, just before 'The Merchant of Venice' was written, also portrays a money-obsessed, revenge-seeking Jew named Barabas; Shakespeare's portrayal of the mercenary Shylock is similar to Marlowe's and reinforced Elizabethan perceptions of Jews.

"I will feed fat the ancient grudge I bear him"

- Shylock clearly states that he plans revenge on Antonio.

- He seems to relish the thought of revenge. The **metaphor** of Shylock feasting on Antonio's suffering is a chilling one and this sinister **image** is enhanced by the soft **alliteration** of **'feed fat'** which creates a sense of unsavoury feasting.

"You call me misbeliever, cut-throat dog, / And spit upon my Jewish gaberdine"

• Shylock reminds Antonio about how he has been appallingly treated by him.

• Antonio has abused Shylock, calling him a **'cut-throat dog'**. By reducing Shylock to the status of an animal, the audience is aware that Shylock is dehumanised. We understand that Shylock has valid reasons for seeking revenge on the man who has openly attacked him.

Context: Christianity was a cornerstone of society in Elizabethan England and Antonio's lack of religious tolerance would not be as shocking for Shakespeare's audience as it is for a modern audience. Yet maybe all audiences would wonder whether there is any justice at the end, when Antonio is never brought to account for his dreadful treatment of Shylock.

"My daughter! O my ducats! O my daughter! Fled with a Christian!"

• Shylock is devastated when his daughter, Jessica, takes his money and runs away with Lorenzo.

• The **exclamatory minor sentences** capture his deep pain at his loss.

• It is arguable as to whether Shylock's anguish is due to losing his daughter or his money. Depending on the production, the actor can emphasise the unhappy father or the unhappy businessman.

Context: Jewish descent is traced through the females in the Jewish family. Jessica marrying outside her religion and converting to Christianity is a disaster for Shylock as it means the Jewish bloodline ends with him.

- Shylock challenges the Venetians to see him as a human being rather than a despised animal.

- The powerful *rhetorical questions*, fired out in quick succession, force the characters, and the audience, to question how they view the persecuted Jews.

- Shakespeare asks us to answer the questions, and there is no other conclusion than yes, that the Jews do feel pain and happiness.

Grade 9 Exploration:
Look at the character in a different way

Is Shylock a victim or villain?

Villain: Shylock's bloodthirsty revenge is compelling and chilling viewing. In Act 4, Bassanio asks Shylock **'why dost thou whet thy knife so earnestly?'** Visually, the grisly collection of the bond is imminent and Shylock's deep desire to maim is clear in the *adverb* **'earnestly'** which shows his enthusiasm in sharpening his knife. Most audiences would be repelled by this graphic display of brutality and see Shylock as the villain of the play at this point. Shakespeare used conventions of Elizabethan drama to structure his comedy so that, by the end of the play, conflict is resolved, the characters are romantically paired and the villain is defeated. 'The Merchant of Venice' follows this structure and Shylock, the obvious villain, loses all power.

Victim: Shylock is relentlessly victimised throughout the play. He is called **'cur'**, **'cruel devil'**, **'inhuman wretch'**; the range of vicious insults are levelled directly at him and explain, if not excuse, his deep desire for revenge. At the end of the play, Shylock loses everything: his wealth, his family, even his religion. Isolated, humiliated and silenced, he arouses huge *pathos* (pity) in the audience as he utters his last words of the play: **'I pray you, give me leave to go from hence; I am not well'**. The audience sees him diminished and incredibly vulnerable and as such, he becomes the victim of the play.

Shylock

Shylock is seen as calculating and the audience immediately associates him with money and business.

'Three thousand ducats; well'

Shylock is a clever businessman.

Shylock relishes the thought of revenge. The *metaphor* of Shylock feasting on Antonio's suffering is a chilling one and the sinister *image* is enhanced by the soft *alliteration* of 'feed fat'.

'I will feed fat the ancient grudge I bear him'

Shylock seeks revenge on Antonio.

Shylock is treated appallingly by the Christians.

'If you prick us, do we not bleed?'

His powerful *rhetorical question* challenges the characters and the audience to see the Jews as humans, not as a sub-species.

Is Shylock a villain or a victim?

Villain: Shylock's bloodthirsty revenge is chilling to an audience as they watch him sharpening his knife in the courtroom.

Victim: Shylock is constantly abused. He is called 'cur' 'cruel devil' and Antonio spits on him. At the end, he has nothing.

Sample GCSE Exam Question

Read the following extract from Act 2 Scene 5.
Answer both questions below the text.
At this point in the play, Shylock is preparing to leave Jessica in charge of the house as he goes for dinner with Bassanio.

SHYLOCK
I am bid forth to supper, Jessica:
There are my keys. But wherefore should I go?
I am not bid for love; they flatter me:
But yet I'll go in hate, to feed upon
The prodigal Christian. Jessica, my girl,
Look to my house. I am right loath to go:
There is some ill a-brewing towards my rest,
For I did dream of money-bags to-night.
LAUNCELOT
I beseech you, sir, go: my young master doth expect
your reproach.
SHYLOCK
So do I his.
LAUNCELOT
An they have conspired together, I will not say you
shall see a masque; but if you do, then it was not

for nothing that my nose fell a-bleeding on
Black-Monday last at six o'clock i' the morning,
falling out that year on Ash-Wednesday was four
year, in the afternoon.
SHYLOCK
What, are there masques? Hear you me, Jessica:
Lock up my doors; and when you hear the drum
And the vile squealing of the wry-neck'd fife,
Clamber not you up to the casements then,
Nor thrust your head into the public street
To gaze on Christian fools with varnish'd faces,
But stop my house's ears, I mean my casements:
Let not the sound of shallow foppery enter
My sober house. By Jacob's staff, I swear,
I have no mind of feasting forth to-night:
But I will go. Go you before me, sirrah;
Say I will come.

a) Write about how Shylock is presented in this extract.

b) Write about how Shylock is presented in the play as a whole.

Sample GCSE Answer

 Start with the point that Shylock is a concerned father

In this extract, Shylock is uneasy, unsettled by his nightmares, **'for I did dream of money-bags to-night'**. He, like many Elizabethans did, sees his dreams as premonitions of the future and there is *dramatic irony* for we, the audience, know that he has good reason to worry. Jessica is planning her escape that night and our knowledge makes us pity the worried Shylock. He speaks to Jessica, addressing her as **'my girl'**; this endearment shows a level of trust and affection which she promptly betrays. Later in the play, we see his devastation at this betrayal as he cries **'my daughter! O my ducats! O my daughter! Fled with a Christian!'** The *exclamatory minor sentences* reflect his deep pain at his loss and this is understandable. Jewish descent is traced through the females in the Jewish family and for Jessica to marry outside her religion and convert to Christianity would have been a disaster for Shylock as it would mean the end of his bloodline.

☑ Explore whether Shylock is concerned about his daughter or his wealth

Yet, arguably, Shylock is not so much worried about his daughter as his wealth. His cries for **'my daughter'** are broken up with cries for **'o my ducats'**. Depending on the production, the actor can emphasise the unhappy father or the unhappy businessman. In the extract, Shylock commands Jessica to **'look to my house'**. The *imperative verb* shows his control over her and reinforces how important it is that she has a care of the house and its contents, guarding his wealth. This concern over money is clear from the outset of the the play as Shylock muses on the amount of money that Antonio wishes to borrow: **'three thousand ducats; well'.** These are Shylock's first words of the play so immediately we associate Shylock with money and business. The way he **repeats** the sum creates a sense of greed around Shylock and the **interjection 'well'** suggests that he is musing on the prospect of making more money. Shakespeare's audience would not have been familiar with Jews as Jews had been expelled from England in 1290. However, Christopher Marlowe's play, 'The Jew of Malta', performed in 1592, also portrays a money-obsessed, revenge-seeking Jew named Barabas; Shakespeare's portrayal of the mercenary Shylock is similar to Marlowe's and reinforced Elizabethan perceptions of Jews. Shylock's concern over protecting his wealth reinforces these perceptions.

✓ Move to the point that Shylock is a man who is constantly under threat

Shylock's anxiety is evident as he queries **'what, are there masques?'** and then issues a series of instructions to keep his family and house safe. He is right to be anxious; in Venice, Jews were confined to a ghetto and subject to different laws from the Christians who despised them. A rowdy masque could easily end in trouble with the Jewish community being targeted for violent sport. This Christian violence to the Jews is also evident in Act 1 when Shylock reminds Antonio about how he has been appallingly treated by him: **'you call me misbeliever, cut-throat dog, And spit upon my Jewish gaberdine'.** By reducing Shylock to the status of an animal, the audience is aware that Shylock is dehumanised and we understand why Shylock has no faith in the Christians in his city as he prepares to leave his house.

✓ Move to the point that Shylock is a man full of vengeance and hate

Shylock is understandably a man full of vengeance and hate; he says that he will **'go in hate'** to Bassanio's dinner. His **declarative statement** leaves us in no doubt of his dark emotions, and the power of these is emphasised by the punched out **monosyllabic** words. This hatred is evident earlier in the play when Shylock clearly states that he plans revenge on Antonio, that '**I will feed fat the ancient grudge I bear him**'. He seems to relish the thought of revenge. The **metaphor** of Shylock feasting on Antonio's suffering is a chilling one and this sinister **image** is enhanced by the soft **alliteration** of **'feed fat'** which captures a sense of indulgent feasting; this repulsive idea is echoed in the extract as Shylock states that he will **'feed upon the prodigal Christian'.** It is interesting to question whether the hatred partly stems from fear of the treatment of Jews by the Christians and certainly his last speech in the extract is **structured** as a string of urgent, fearful instructions, peppered with **imperative verbs**: **'hear' 'lock' 'stop'.** Yet Shylock's words also seem to suggest that his hatred is based more on contempt than fear as he says '**let not the sound of shallow foppery enter my sober house'.** The **juxtaposition** of **'shallow'** to describe the Christians with **'sober'** to describe himself highlights how Shylock views himself as superior; he is God-fearing and solemn while the Christians are shallow and foolish. His hatred is based perhaps on a range of emotions: fear and revenge but also disdain.

✓ Finish by exploring whether Shylock is a villain or a victim

Shylock's bloodthirsty revenge is compelling and chilling viewing. In Act 4, Bassanio asks Shylock **'why dost thou whet thy knife so earnestly?'** Visually, the grisly collection of the bond is imminent and Shylock's deep desire to maim is clear in the **adverb 'earnestly'** which shows his enthusiasm in sharpening his knife. Most audiences would be repelled by this graphic display of brutality and see Shylock as the villain of the play at this point. Shakespeare used conventions of Elizabethan drama to structure his comedy so that, by the end of the play, conflict is resolved, the characters are romantically paired and the villain is defeated. 'The Merchant of Venice' follows this **structure** as Shylock, the obvious villain, loses all power. Yet Shylock can also be seen as a victim. Shylock is relentlessly victimised throughout the play. He is called **'cur', 'cruel devil'** and '**inhuman wretch'**; the range of vicious insults are levelled directly at him and explain, if not excuse, his deep desire for revenge. At the end of the play, Shylock loses everything: his wealth, his family, even his religion. Isolated, humiliated and silenced, he arouses huge **pathos** in the audience as he utters his last words of the play: **'I pray you, give me leave to go from hence; I am not well'.** The audience sees him diminished and incredibly vulnerable and as such, he becomes the victim of the play.

5 Jessica
Character analysis

Jessica is Shylock's daughter who steals from her father and elopes with her Christian lover, Lorenzo. Whether she is motivated by love or by other emotions is open to interpretation.

"Our house is hell"

- Jessica decides to leave her unhappy household and marry Lorenzo.

- Her unhappiness is clearly revealed through the **metaphor** comparing her home to hell. Rather than passively suffer, Jessica takes control of her own life and escapes with Lorenzo. The **declarative sentence** reflects her rejection of her home.

Context: In Venice, the Jewish community were forced to live by law in a segregated part of the city called a ghetto. They were treated badly by the Christian rulers. Jessica's desire to leave her home and become Lorenzo's wife might well be founded in a desire for a better life rather than deep love for Lorenzo.

"Lorenzo, certain, and my love indeed"

- Jessica checks that it is Lorenzo who is come, disguised in a mask, to take her from Shylock's house.

- Love is seen as passionate and joyful as Jessica and Lorenzo are united, able to transcend the race boundaries that divide Venetian society. The words **'certain'** and **'indeed'** captures how deep and committed her love is.

- Jessica's love affair is also used by Shakespeare as a **plot device**. Jessica's escape with her lover devastates Shylock and increases his desire for revenge.

"But though I am a daughter to his blood, I am not to his manners"

- Jessica rejects her father and therefore her religion.

- The audience sees her internal conflict; she lives in a family and a community that does not suit her.

Context: Jewish descent is traced through the females in the Jewish family. For Jessica to marry outside her religion and convert to Christianity would have been a disaster for Shylock as it would mean the end of the bloodline. Jessica would have known this.

"A ring he had of your daughter for a monkey"

- Shylock hears reports about how Jessica and her new husband are spending huge amounts of money, and how Jessica has sold her mother's ring.

- The reports present Jessica as a spendthrift. This might be a way of celebrating escape after living for years with the financially-astute Shylock.

- The way she sells the ring which has great sentimental value suggests that she is callous. Certainly, Shylock's pain at this news can shift the audience's response so that we lose sympathy with her.

"I am never merry when I hear sweet music"

- In Act 5, Jessica seems sad despite the pretty music.

- Jessica's last words of the play are significant, suggesting that, far from being a joyous bride, she is already melancholy.

- Lorenzo's long speech encouraging her to enjoy the music could easily be seen as Lorenzo dominating and silencing his new wife. It is possible that Jessica is realising that she has swapped one restricted life for another.

Context: Shakespeare followed the classic five act structure from Greek theatre which ended in resolution for the characters yet Jessica's last words seem to indicate that there is possibly no happy ending for her.

Grade 9 Exploration:
Look at the character in a different way

How far is Jessica motivated by love?

Love: Jessica is a girl swept up in the strong emotion that is passionate love. The banter between Jessica and Lorenzo in Act Five reflects a closeness and a merry companionship. They play on each other's words, each adding to the phrase **'in such a night'** and comparing it to nights in which famous lovers met. For example, **'in such a night/ Troilus methinks mounted the Troyan walls'**. Shakespeare uses the moonlit night as a traditional *setting* for the lovers in Act Five, reinforcing the passion and romance of their relationship.

The ideal of courtly love was revived in the Elizabethan era. It was the idealistic and noble admiration of lovers for each other with references to Greek mythology. Lorenzo and Jessica's conversation represent this literary tradition, and highlight the pure and uplifting nature of their love.

Other emotions: There are potentially stronger drivers than love for Jessica. Her household does not make her happy and we see Shylock order her to **'lock up my doors'** when he goes out for dinner. The *imperative verb* shows how he controls her and his concern appears to be for his household wealth not his daughter. The atmosphere does not seem a pleasant one and Jessica is twisted with internal conflict that she seeks to end by marrying Lorenzo and becoming **'a Christian and a loving wife'**. Interestingly, she places Christianity as her first reason for eloping, the position of wife comes second. This perhaps reflects the reasons behind her marriage; escaping to become a Christian and therefore becoming a first class citizen is more important than her love for Lorenzo.

Essential Exam Tips

☑ If you can use correct literary terminology (metaphor/imperative verbs etc), do use it! It makes your response much more convincing.

☑ Spend 5 minutes planning your answer; this helps you organise your ideas into a structure that is clear for the examiner.

Jessica's internal conflict is clear; she does not fit into the community into which she was born.

Her passionate love for Lorenzo transcends the racial divide of Venetian society.

'But though I am a daughter to his blood, I am not to his manners'

'Lorenzo certain and my love indeed'

Jessica is a girl in turmoil.

Jessica is a girl in love.

Jessica

Jessica is perhaps not completely happy at the end.

Is Jessica motivated by love?

'I am never merry when I hear sweet music'

Yes: Jessica is passionately in love and her banter with Lorenzo in Act Five as they both add to the phrase **'in such a night'** reflects their closeness.

Jessica is melancholy despite the beautiful night and her recent wedding; perhaps disillusionment is already setting in.

No: Jessica is motivated by a desire to be a Christian before she is a **'loving wife'**. Segregated from Venetian society by her religion, she sees the marriage as a way of gaining acceptance in society.

Read the following extract from Act 2 Scene 6.
Answer both questions below the text.

At this point in the play, Jessica is preparing to run away with Lorenzo.'

Enter JESSICA, above, in boy's clothes
JESSICA
Who are you? Tell me, for more certainty,
Albeit I'll swear that I do know your tongue.
LORENZO
Lorenzo, and thy love.
JESSICA
Lorenzo, certain, and my love indeed,
For who love I so much? And now who knows
But you, Lorenzo, whether I am yours?
LORENZO
Heaven and thy thoughts are witness that thou art.
JESSICA
Here, catch this casket; it is worth the pains.
I am glad 'tis night, you do not look on me,
For I am much ashamed of my exchange:
But love is blind and lovers cannot see
The pretty follies that themselves commit;
For if they could, Cupid himself would blush

To see me thus transformed to a boy.
LORENZO
Descend, for you must be my torchbearer.
JESSICA
What, must I hold a candle to my shames?
They in themselves, good-sooth, are too too light.
Why, 'tis an office of discovery, love;
And I should be obscured.
LORENZO
So are you, sweet,
Even in the lovely garnish of a boy.
But come at once;
For the close night doth play the runaway,
And we are stay'd for at Bassanio's feast.
JESSICA
I will make fast the doors, and gild myself
With some more ducats, and be with you straight.

a) How is Jessica presented in this extract?

b) How is Jessica presented in the play as a whole?

☑ Start with the point that Jessica is a woman who is anxious and on edge

In the extract, Jessica is full of anxiety. She leans out of her window to ask **'who are you?'** of the men waiting. The ***interrogative sentence structure*** reflects her unease as does her demand for the men to reveal their identity: **'tell me, for more certainty'**. Her anxiety is understandable; it is night-time and the men are disguised in masks, and she is about to leave the safety of her family home. Yet by the end of the extract, she is reassured and is decisive; **'I will make fast the doors... and be with you straight'**. Her ***declarative sentences*** show that the earlier unease is gone and the ***modal verb*** **'will'** suggests a firm determination to escape.

☑ Move to the point that she is intent on escape

This determination to escape from Shylock's house is clear from the ***stage directions*** which has the actor playing **'in boy's clothes'**. Jessica is clearly uncomfortable about the disguise as she says **'I am glad 'tis night, you do not look on me'** but nevertheless is so keen to leave her family home that she puts on the boy's clothes. This is in part a ***plot device*** to engage the audience and Shakespeare often used disguises, popular in Greek theatre, to add to the ***dramatic tension*** of his plays. Here the men in masks and the girl in a boy's outfit adds to the exciting drama of the escape and entertains the audience.

Move to the point that Jessica is passionately in love

The reason for this determined desire to escape is her love for Lorenzo. We see a girl head over heels in love as as she takes Lorenzo's words **'Lorenzo, and thy love'** and twists them to **'Lorenzo, certain, and my love indeed'**. The words **'certain'** and **'indeed'** reflect how deep and committed her love is, and the audience is caught up in their romance. Their love is all the more exciting because of their backgrounds. The Jewish community in Renaissance Venice was forced to live in a segregated part of the city and were treated as second class citizens. Jessica and Lorenzo's love is seen as able to transcend the race boundaries that divide Venetian society. This deep love is shown again in the banter between Jessica and Lorenzo in Act 5 which reflects their closeness and merry companionship. They play on each other's words, each adding to the phrase **'in such a night'**, comparing it to nights in which famous lovers met, for example, **'in such a night Troilus methinks mounted the Troyan walls'**. Shakespeare uses the moonlit night as a traditional setting for the lovers in Act Five, reinforcing the passion and romance of their relationship. The ideal of courtly love was revived in the Elizabethan era. This was the idealistic and noble admiration of lovers for each other and often referred to Greek mythology. Lorenzo and Jessica's conversation represent this literary tradition, and highlight the pure and uplifting nature of their love.

 ### Move on to explore her other motives for escaping

Yet there are potentially stronger drivers than love for Jessica. Her household does not make her happy as she describes it as **'hell'** and we see Shylock order her to **'lock up my doors'** when he goes out for dinner. The *imperative verb* shows how he controls her and his concern seems to be for his household wealth not his daughter. The atmosphere does not seem a pleasant one and Jessica is twisted with internal conflict that she seeks to end by marrying Lorenzo and becoming **'a Christian and a loving wife'**. Interestingly, she places Christianity as her first reason for eloping, the position of wife comes second. This perhaps reflects the reasons behind her marriage; escaping to become a Christian and therefore becoming a first-class citizen is more important than her love for Lorenzo.

 ### Finish by exploring whether she is a sympathetic character

Jessica can be viewed as a sympathetic character; certainly, her internal conflict is clear as she earlier states **'but though I am a daughter to his blood/I am not to his manners'**. She lives in a family and a community that does not suit her and so she is forced to reject her father and therefore her religion. Yet her escape with her lover devastates Shylock. Jewish descent is traced through the females in the Jewish family and for Jessica to marry outside her religion and convert to Christianity would have been a disaster for Shylock as it means an end to his Jewish bloodline. We see the pain she inflicts and this can temper our sympathetic response, as can her mercenary attitude. In this extract, she seems materialistic as she throws down a box full of money to Lorenzo, telling him to **'catch this casket; it is worth the pains'**. She uses a matter-of-fact *tone* of voice that suggests that she is thinking about financial security rather than being overwhelmed with love. Yet perhaps she is simply realistic, aware that she needs to bring money with her to help the start of their marriage, or perhaps she is painfully aware that part of her appeal to Lorenzo is the money she brings with her. This is illustrated when, at the end of the extract, she disappears inside to **'gild myself/With some more ducats'**. The *verb* **'gild'** means to cover thinly with gold; Jessica deliberately positions herself as a bride shining with gold and so financially attractive, ensuring Lorenzo will see past her despised Jewish background. Perhaps her obsession with money is based on a need for security yet later in the play, Shylock hears reports about how Jessica and Lorenzo are spending huge amounts of money, and how Jessica has sold her mother's ring: **'a ring he had of your daughter for a monkey'**. The reports show Jessica to be a spendthrift, and the way she sells the ring which has great sentimental value suggests that she is callous. Certainly, Shylock's pain at this news shifts the audience's response so that we lcan ose sympathy with her. However, at the end, we see her melancholy as she states **'I am never merry when I hear sweet music'**; her marriage does not seem to be bringing her happiness and perhaps life as a Christian is not everything she expected it to be. An audience might well feel pity for the reckless girl who risked everything for a better life and did not find it.

6 Lorenzo
Character analysis

Lorenzo is the passionate Venetian who elopes with Jessica, illustrating how true love can overcome religious prejudice.

> "O Lorenzo, if thou keep promise, I shall end this strife/ Become a Christian and thy loving wife"

• Jessica plans to elope with Lorenzo.

• Lorenzo is seen as a saviour, someone who will rescue Jessica from her hellish household.

• He is in part a *plot device*; the drama of the escape is highly entertaining for the audience and Jessica's betrayal devastates Shylock and increases his desire for revenge.

• The *conditional 'if'* suggests that Jessica is not entirely convinced about Lorenzo's intentions. There is a suggestion that he is not trustworthy.

Context: In Venice, the Jewish community were forced to live by law in a segregated part of the city called a ghetto. They were treated badly by the Christian rulers. Jessica's desire to leave her home and become Lorenzo's wife might well be founded in a desire for a better life rather than deep love for Lorenzo.

> "Gold and jewels she is furnish'd with"

• Lorenzo says that Jessica will come to him with her father's **'gold and jewels'**.

• Lorenzo is, perhaps, an opportunistic adventurer. He seems delighted that his bride will be bringing so much wealth.

Context: In the 16th century, marriages were often based at least in part on financial considerations. Women were expected to bring a dowry (sum of money) to their marriage. Lorenzo's expectation that his new wife will bring wealth to the marriage was one that Shakespeare's audience would have understood.

"For she is wise, if I can judge of her"

- Lorenzo muses on Jessica's virtues and good qualities.

- He values her intelligence, calling her **'wise'**. His respect for her bodes well for this marriage.

- Yet the **conditional 'if'** could suggest that he does not know her. Indeed, the nature of Venetian society with Jessica in the Jewish ghetto and Lorenzo living with the Christians does mean that it is unlikely that the lovers have ever spent much time together.

"A ring he had of your daughter for a monkey"

- Tubal tells Shylock that Lorenzo and Jessica spend huge amounts of money in Genoa and it seems that they are soon reduced to selling Jessica's jewellery.

- Lorenzo seems reckless and a spendthrift; the audience might well wonder if he will make Jessica happy.

"Did pretty Jessica, like a little shrew, Slander her love, and he forgave it her"

- Lorenzo talks with Jessica in the moonlit garden at Belmont. Their banter shows a closeness and a merry companionship. They play on each other's words, each adding to the phrase **'in such a night'**.

- Yet there might be an edge to this banter which could indicate that the characters are trying to seize an advantage over each other. Also, the **simile 'like a little shrew'** could be playful yet it could indicate that Lorenzo is not happy with his bride and there are already cracks in their relationship.

Grade 9 Exploration:
Look at the character in a different way

Is Lorenzo a man who is genuinely in love?

Yes: Shakespeare presents a man who is passionately in love. Despite the suspicion that Lorenzo and Jessica have barely met, there is no doubting the genuine nature of their emotions and, indeed, Shakespeare often created couples who fell in love instantly, Romeo and Juliet being the most famous example. The final scene where the lovers play on each other's words using the phrase **'in such a night'** shows their harmony as they compare it to nights in which famous lovers met: for example, **'in such a night/ Troilus methinks mounted the Troyan walls'**. Shakespeare uses the moonlit night as a traditionally romantic *setting* for the lovers in Act V, reinforcing the passion and romance of their relationship.

The ideal of courtly love was revived in the Elizabethan era. It was the idealistic and noble admiration of lovers for each other and often referred to Greek mythology. Lorenzo and Jessica's conversation represents this literary tradition, and shows the pure and uplifting nature of their love. Yet all the lovers that they refer to, such as Troilus and Cressida, were relationships that ended in betrayal and tragedy. Perhaps Jessica and Lorenzo already view their relationship as one that is also doomed.

No: In Act 5, Jessica seems sad despite the pretty music, saying **'I am never merry when I hear sweet music'**. Her last words of the play are significant as they suggest that, far from being a joyous bride, she is already melancholy. Lorenzo's subsequent long speech encouraging her to enjoy the music could easily be seen as a pompous attempt by Lorenzo to dominate and silence his new wife. Ultimately, Lorenzo took his wife in a sly, deceitful way from her father's house, spent all her money in a few days in Genoa and is now dominating her. Their relationship appears to be floundering.

Essential Exam Tips

☑ Don't spend ages writing an introduction. Get stuck into the question straightaway.

☑ Keep an eye on the time. Write the time that you need to have finished this Shakespeare question on a piece of paper and stick to it. If you run over too much, your response to the next question will suffer.

The passionate love of Lorenzo and Jessica transcends the racial divide of Venetian society.

Lorenzo is delighted that his wife will bring **'gold and jewels'**. He is maybe not so much a man in love but an adventurer.

'Lorenzo certain and my love indeed'

'gold and jewels'

Lorenzo is a man who is deeply in love.

Lorenzo is, perhaps, motivated by greed.

Lorenzo

Lorenzo is reckless.

Is Lorenzo a man who is genuinely in love?

'a ring he had of your daughter for a monkey'

Yes: His last scene is with Jessica in the romantic moonlit garden in Belmont. They show their harmony through the *wordplay* on **'on such a night'**.

Lorenzo and Jessica soon spend all of their money in Genoa. There is little preparation for their future.

No: Lorenzo's relationship is already showing cracks. Jessica is melancholy and his long speech encouraging her to be happy seems dominating and controlling.

Read the following extract from Act 5 Scene 1.
Answer both questions below the text.
At this point in the play, Lorenzo and Jessica are in the house at Belmont, waiting Portia's return.

LORENZO
In such a night
Stood Dido with a willow in her hand
Upon the wild sea banks and waft her love
To come again to Carthage.
JESSICA
In such a night
Medea gather'd the enchanted herbs
That did renew old AEson.
LORENZO
In such a night
Did Jessica steal from the wealthy Jew
And with an unthrift love did run from Venice

As far as Belmont.
JESSICA
In such a night
Did young Lorenzo swear he loved her well,
Stealing her soul with many vows of faith
And ne'er a true one.
LORENZO
In such a night
Did pretty Jessica, like a little shrew,
Slander her love, and he forgave it her.
JESSICA
I would out-night you, did no body come;
But, hark, I hear the footing of a man.

a) Write about how Lorenzo is presented in this extract.
b) Write about how Lorenzo is presented in the play as a whole.

 Sample GCSE Answer

 Make the point that Lorenzo is presented as a man in love

In this extract, Shakespeare presents a man who is passionately in love. This final scene where the lovers play on each other's words using the phrase **'in such a night'** shows their harmony as they take it in turns to compare it to nights in which famous lovers met: for example, **'in such a night Medea gather'd the enchanted herbs/That did renew old Aeson'**. Shakespeare uses the moonlit night as a traditionally romantic *setting* for the lovers in Act Five, reinforcing the passion and romance of their relationship. The ideal of courtly love was revived in the Elizabethan era; it was the idealistic and noble admiration of lovers for each other and often made reference to Greek mythology. Lorenzo and Jessica's conversation, referring to Medea and Dido and Carthage, represents this literary tradition; it also shows the pure and uplifting nature of their love and reaffirms our impression of Lorenzo as a man head over heels in love. His language is highly elevated at first, with the *alliteration* in **'a willow in her hand/Upon the wild sea banks and waft'** capturing a gentle, poignant sense of strong, noble emotions.

☑ Explore how Lorenzo is presented as a hero who saves Jessica

This deep love that the couple experiences is evident earlier in the play when Jessica checks that it is Lorenzo who has come, disguised in a mask, to take her from Shylock's house, exclaiming **'Lorenzo certain, and my love indeed'**. Love is seen as passionate and joyful as Jessica and Lorenzo are united. The words **'certain'** and **'indeed'** capture how deep and committed their love is, and the audience is caught up in their romance.

Despite the suspicion that Lorenzo and Jessica have barely met, their emotions seem genuine, and, indeed, Shakespeare often created couples who fell in love instantly, Romeo and Juliet being the most famous example. Lorenzo is also in part a ***plot device***; the drama of the escape is highly entertaining for the audience and Jessica's betrayal devastates Shylock and increases his desire for revenge. Yet perhaps Lorenzo is best seen as a hero; he rescues Jessica from her hellish household, his love transcending the racial divides that kept Jessica in the Jewish ghetto away from Christians like himself.

☑ Move to the point that Lorenzo is reckless

However, Lorenzo is not a perfect hero for Jessica. Shakespeare often created young men in love who were reckless, and Lorenzo is certainly this. He refers to himself as an **'unthrift love'**, acknowledging that he is foolish with money. The audience has already heard evidence of this from Tubal and Shylock's conversation about how the runaway lovers have spent huge amounts of money in Genoa. Tubal tells how Jessica sold her mother's ring for **'a monkey'**, implying that Lorenzo and Jessica have run out of money and are reduced to selling Jessica's jewelry. Lorenzo seems reckless and a spendthrift; the audience might well wonder if he will make Jessica a suitable husband.

☑ Start to explore whether Lorenzo is a man who will be a good husband

This uncertainty as to whether Lorenzo will make Jessica happy is reinforced elsewhere in the extract. The lovers' conversation could be played as humorous banter yet there are undercurrents that can unsettle an audience. Jessica says that Lorezo is deceitful, **'stealing her soul with many vows of faith/And ne'er a true one'**. Indeed, there is truth in the charge of theft; Lorenzo did take her from her father's house in the darkness of night, disguised in a mask. There is a sense of dishonesty which underpins their relationship, and perhaps Jessica suspected this from the beginning. When thinking of Lorenzo in Act 2, she says **'O Lorenzo, if thou keep promise/I shall end this strife/Become a Christian and a loving wife'**. The ***conditional*** 'if' suggests that Jessica is not entirely convinced about Lorenzo's intentions. There is a suggestion that he is not trustworthy even from the opening of the play.

☑ Continue to explore Lorenzo's motivations

Yet Lorenzo was always intent on marrying Jessica; what lies open to question is whether he marries her for love. Lorenzo says in Act Two that Jessica will come to him with her father's **'gold and jewels'**, suggesting that he is, perhaps, an opportunistic adventurer. He seem delighted that his bride will be bringing so much wealth. However, in the 16th century, marriages were often based at least in part on financial considerations and women were expected to bring a dowry (sum of money) to their marriage. Lorenzo's expectation that his new wife will bring wealth to the marriage was one that Shakespeare's audience would have understood. Yet whatever his motivation in marrying, he does not convince us that he is making Jessica happy. In the extract, the continual play on **'in such a night'** might not be gentle harmony but rather sharp banter which could indicate that the characters are trying to seize the advantage. Furthermore, the ***simile*** **'like a little shrew'** could be playful yet it could have an edge, suggesting that Lorenzo is not happy with his bride. Later in Act Five, Jessica seems sad despite the pretty music, saying **'I am never merry when I hear sweet music'**. Her last words of the play are significant as they suggest that, far from being a joyous bride, she is already melancholy and Lorenzo's subsequent long speech encouraging her to enjoy the music could easily be seen as a pompous attempt by Lorenzo dominating and silencing his new wife. Indeed, in their banter, all the lovers that they refer to, such as Troilus and Cressida, were relationships that ended in betrayal and tragedy. Perhaps Jessica and Lorenzo already view their relationship as one that is also doomed. Ultimately, Lorenzo took his wife in a sly, deceitful way from her father's house, spent all her money in a few days in Genoa and is now dominating her. He is not necessarily an attractive character; directors and actors can present him in many different ways.

The desire for wealth is a motivator for many of the characters in the play and drives the plot throughout.

"Her sunny locks/ Hang on her temples like a golden fleece"

- Bassanio describes Portia as a beautiful woman whose blonde hair resembles a golden fleece.

- The **simile** shows that he is interested in her in terms of her appearance and her wealth. The golden fleece refers to the Greek myth in which Jason and his crew of Argonauts sailed in a quest which had the golden fleece as the prize.

Context: In the 16th century, marriages were often based at least in part on financial considerations. Women were expected to bring a dowry (sum of money) to their marriage. The way that Bassanio is interested in Portia as a prize suggests that he is motivated by her potential dowry rather than love.

"Three thousand ducats; well"

- Shylock muses on the amount of money that Antonio wishes to borrow.

- These are Shylock's first words of the play. Immediately, we associate Shylock with money.

- The way he **repeats** the sum creates a sense of greed around Shylock and the **interjection** 'well' suggests that he is musing on the prospect of making more money.

Context: Shakespeare's audience would not have been familiar with Jews as Jews had been expelled from England in 1290. However, Christopher Marlowe's play, 'The Jew of Malta', performed in 1592, also portrays a money-obsessed, revenge-seeking Jew named Barabas; Shakespeare's portrayal of the mercenary Shylock is similar to Marlowe's and reinforced Elizabethan perceptions of Jews.

"He lends out money gratis and brings down/ The rate of usance here with us in Venice"

- Shylock states that one of the reasons for his hatred for Antonio is the way that Antonio lends money without interest.

- Desire for wealth is seen as a cause for conflict and also drives the plot. There is deep resentment between Antonio and Shylock because of the financial regulations.

Context: Venice's laws were divisive as only Jews were allowed to charge interest on loaned money. Prejudice was cemented in the society through the unequal financial laws.

"All my fortunes are at sea"
"Dangerous rocks...enrobe the roaring waters with my silks"

- Antonio admits that he has no spare money as he waits for his merchant ships to return to Venice. There are plenty of references in the play to the perils of sea journeys.

- Money is seen to be fickle; there is a sense of uncertainty and risk associated with business.

- The *metaphor* highlights the treacherous nature of the boats' journeys. The *adjectives* **'dangerous'** and **'roaring'** emphasise the vicious nature of the sea which can easily destroy the fragile boats and their cargo.

Context: Venice was one of the great trading ports of Europe and Shakespeare's audience was aware of its reputation as a place where enormous wealth was generated. Yet they were also aware of the perilous nature of sea journeys and so a sense of unease is created as Antonio pledges to return money which he does not yet have.

> **"Superfluity comes sooner by white hairs, but competency lives longer"**

- Nerissa gives Portia sensible advice, reminding her that excess living ages us and that to have just enough money means a longer, healthier life.

- Shakespeare uses Nerissa to remind the audience that desire for wealth can be damaging.

Grade 9 Exploration:
Look at the theme in a different way

Is the desire for wealth at the root of all of the relationships?

Yes: All of the love relationships are based on financial gain. Bassanio becomes engaged to Portia using the language of a financial transaction as he says that their engagement must be **'confirm'd, sign'd, ratified by you'**; each *verb* in the *list* highlights the commercial nature of their love. Jessica only leaves with Lorenzo after she has said that she will **'gild myself/With some more ducats'**, making us wonder whether Lorenzo would be so keen to elope if she did not bring her father's treasure with her. Shylock and Antonio are locked in a feud based on finances and Bassanio plays on Antonio's love for him in order to borrow money. It does indeed seem as if desire for wealth is at the heart of all relationships.

No: There can be little doubt that genuine love between Jessica and Lorenzo is their main motivator, not greed. As they are united at Shylock's house, Jessica cries **'Lorenzo, certain, and my love indeed'**. The use of **'certain'** and **'indeed'** show Jessica's relief and joy, and their utter commitment, as she leaves her home to be Lorenzo's bride. Furthermore, it is not really financial greed that drives the **'pound of flesh'** plot; Shylock's hatred for Antonio is based on religion, not money. His stark *declarative statement* - **'I hate him for he is a Christian'** - leaves the audience in no doubt about the depth of Shylock's hatred. The reason for this hatred is evident in the sentence construction; the *conjunction* **'for'** links the two *clauses* together and reflects how the hatred is inextricably linked to religion. Greed is a minor motivator compared to the other driving forces in the play.

The *simile* shows that Bassanio is interested in Portia in terms of her appearance and her wealth, not love.

The *adjectives* 'dangerous' and 'roaring' emphasise the vicious nature of the sea which can easily destroy the fragile boats and their cargo.

'her sunny locks
Hang on her temples like a golden fleece'

'all my fortunes are at sea' 'dangerous rocks... enrobe the roaring waters with my silks'

Greed is a motivator for the characters.

Wealth is fickle and impermanent.

Wealth & Greed

Wealth causes conflict.

Is the desire for wealth at the root of all relationships?

'He lends out money gratis and brings down/ The rate of usance here with us in Venice'

Yes: Portia's wealth motivates Bassanio, Jessica elopes only when **'gild(ed) with ducats'** and Shylock's feud with Antonio stems from different methods of business.

There is resentment between Antonio and Shylock because of Venice's financial regulation which only allowed Jews to charge
interest on loaned money.

No: Love and hate are the two most powerful motivators in the play, not greed.

Read the following extract from Act 1 Scene 3.
Answer both questions below the text.
At this point in the play, Shylock is manipulating Antonio into agreeing to the terms of the three thousand ducat loan.

SHYLOCK
Why, look you, how you storm!
I would be friends with you and have your love,
Forget the shames that you have stain'd me with,
Supply your present wants and take no doit
Of usance for my moneys, and you'll not hear me:
This is kind I offer.
BASSANIO
This were kindness.
SHYLOCK
This kindness will I show.
Go with me to a notary, seal me there
Your single bond; and, in a merry sport,
If you repay me not on such a day,
In such a place, such sum or sums as are

Express'd in the condition, let the forfeit
Be nominated for an equal pound
Of your fair flesh, to be cut off and taken
In what part of your body pleaseth me.
ANTONIO
Content, i' faith: I'll seal to such a bond
And say there is much kindness in the Jew.
BASSANIO
You shall not seal to such a bond for me:
I'll rather dwell in my necessity.
ANTONIO
Why, fear not, man; I will not forfeit it:
Within these two months, that's a month before
This bond expires, I do expect return
Of thrice three times the value of this bond.

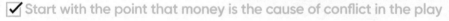

a) Write about how wealth and greed are presented in this extract.
b) Write about how wealth and greed are presented in the play as a whole.

Sample GCSE Answer

☑ Start with the point that money is the cause of conflict in the play

The desire for wealth is a cause of conflict in the play and this is evident at the start of the extract with Antonio losing his temper and causing Shylock to remark **'why, look you, how you storm!'** It is clear that Antonio is furious with Shylock as they argue about the lending of money. This argument has its roots in the divisive laws of Venice which only allowed Jews to lend money and charge interest. This leads to deep resentment between the two as Shylock hates the way that Antonio undermines his business by lending **'out money gratis (which) brings down the rate of usance here with us in Venice'** and Antonio in turn is jealous of the easy money that Shylock makes from the interest. This desire for wealth sparks conflict between the two and so drives the plot towards the dramatic courtroom scene.

☑ Move to the point that wealth is important to the characters

Shylock uses Antonio's need for money as a way of manipulating him. Antonio needs funds to help Bassanio and so is tricked into agreeing to Shylock's loan as Shylock declares the unusual bond as **'a merry sport'**. There is nothing amusing about the idea of a **'pound of... flesh'** being hacked off Antonio's body but Antonio falls straight into Shylock's trap and readily agrees to **'seal to such a bond'**. The audience is far more uneasy; from our introduction to Shylock earlier in the play, we see a man who calculates and plots as Shylock muses on the amount of money that Antonio wishes to borrow, saying **'three thousand ducats; well'.** These are Shylock's first words of the play and, immediately, we associate Shylock with money. This creates a sense of greed around Shylock and the *interjection* **'well'** suggests that he is musing on the prospect of making more money and also using money as a tool with which to exact revenge. Shakespeare's audience would not have been familiar with Jews as Jews had been expelled from England in 1290. However, Christopher Marlowe's play, 'The Jew of Malta', performed in 1592, also portrays a money-obsessed, revenge-seeking Jew named Barabas; Shakespeare's portrayal of the mercenary Shylock is similar to Marlowe's and reinforced Elizabethan perceptions of Jews.

Discuss how wealth is presented as fickle

Antonio is confident that his wealth is safe, telling Bassanio that **'I do expect return/Of thrice three times the value of this bond'**. He looks forward to a financial profit and seems relaxed about the return of the ships. Yet, again, the audience is more uneasy. From the opening scene, we see that Antonio is financially exposed as he admits that **'all my fortunes are at sea'** and an audience might question Antonio's business sense as he states that **'all'** his fortunes are at risk at one time. There are plenty of references throughout the play to the treacherous nature of the boats' journeys; for example, **'dangerous rocks... enrobe the roaring waters with my silks'**. The *adjectives* **'dangerous'** and **'roaring'** emphasise the vicious nature of the sea which can easily destroy the fragile boats and their cargo. Wealth is seen to be precarious; there is a sense of uncertainty and risk associated with business. Venice was one of the great trading ports of Europe and Shakespeare's audience was aware of its reputation as a place where enormous wealth was generated. Yet they were also aware of the perilous nature of sea journeys and so a sense of unease is created in the extract as Antonio pledges to return money which he does not yet have.

Explore where the desire for wealth is at the heart of all relationships

The desire for money drives Antonio and Shylock's relationship and, arguably, all of the relationships in the play. Bassanio's burning desire for wealth is evident as he manipulates Antonio's friendship in order to secure the loan that he cannot get himself and allows Antonio to place himself in mortal danger. This manipulation is evident in the extract when he states **'you shall not seal to such a bond for me: I'll rather dwell in my necessity'**. His *declarative statement* and use of the the *modal verbs* suggest conviction, that Bassanio understands how risky the bond is and will emphatically not allow his friend to endanger himself. Yet Antonio does seal the bond and Bassanio does not say another word, indicating that his love of money is more important than his friend's life. Later, we see Bassanio again as a man who views the world through greedy eyes; as he becomes engaged to Portia, he uses the language of a financial transaction as he says that their engagement must be **'confirm'd, sign'd, ratified by you'**; each *verb* in the *list* highlights the commercial nature of their love. Similarly, Jessica only leaves with Lorenzo after she has been back in the house to **'gild myself/With some more ducats'**, making us wonder whether Lorenzo would be so keen to elope if she did not bring her father's treasure with her. The *verb* **'gild'** means to cover thinly with gold; Jessica deliberately positions herself as a bride shining with gold and so financially attractive, ensuring Lorenzo will see past her despised Jewish background. It does seem as if wealth, not love motivates the characters.

Continue to explore whether greed is really the cornerstone of relationships

Yet this is only one view and surely there can be little doubt that genuine love between Jessica and Lorenzo is their main motivator, not greed. As they are united at Shylock's house, Jessica cries **'Lorenzo, certain, and my love indeed'**. The use of **'certain'** and **'indeed'** show Jessica's relief and joy, and their utter commitment, as she leaves her home to be Lorenzo's bride. Furthermore, it is not really financial greed that drives the **'pound of flesh'** plot; Shylock's hatred for Antonio is based on religion, not money. His stark *declarative statement* - **'I hate him for he is a Christian'** - leaves the audience in no doubt about the depth of Shylock's hatred. The reason for this hatred is evident in the sentence construction; the *conjunction* **'for'** links the two clauses together and reflects how the hatred is inextricably linked to religion. The desire for wealth is certainly an emotion that is universal, yet it is by no means the only or even the strongest motivator of the characters within the play.

'The Merchant of Venice' is a romantic comedy, a genre popular in Elizabethan theatre, with witty lovers who have to overcome barriers in order to be together. Love seems to be celebrated as a driving force that brings much joy to the characters.

> **"Her sunny locks/ Hang on her temples like a golden fleece"**

- Bassanio describes Portia as a beautiful woman whose blonde hair resembles a golden fleece.

- The *simile* shows that he is interested in her in terms of her appearance and her wealth. The golden fleece refers to the Greek myth in which Jason and his crew of Argonauts sailed in a quest which had the golden fleece as the prize.

Context: In the 16th century, women were expected to bring a dowry (sum of money) to their marriage. The way that Bassanio is interested in Portia as a prize suggests that he is motivated by her wealth rather than love.

> **"Never be chosen by any rightly but one who shall rightly love"**

- The casket task has been designed by Portia's father to ensure that only a man who truly loves her will be able to choose the right casket.

- The audience sees paternal love here as Portia's father tries to protect his daughter from an unhappy marriage. Her father was clearly aware of the deceptive nature of love and how the lines between appearance and reality can be blurred.

"Lorenzo, certain, and my love indeed"

- Jessica checks that it is Lorenzo who has come, disguised in a mask, to take her from Shylock's house.

- Love is seen as passionate and joyful as Jessica and Lorenzo are united, able to transcend the race boundaries that divide Venetian society.

- Love is also used by Shakespeare as a *plot device*. Jessica's escape with her love devastates Shylock and increases his desire for revenge.

"This house, these servants and this same myself/Are yours, my lord: I give them with this ring"

- Portia consents to marry Bassanio.

- Love is seen here in terms of submission of power. Portia acknowledges that she is giving herself entirely to Bassanio.

- The *list* emphasises that she is giving everything; interestingly, she places herself as the last item in the *list*, implying that the material possessions are of more interest.

Context: In the 16th century, women were the property of their husbands. They had no legal rights and could not own property; Portia's words may seem generous and selfless yet they also reflect the stark reality of the situation as she, and all of her property and wealth, does indeed belong to Bassanio.

"You shall see how much I was a braggart"

- Love changes Bassanio from the overconfident youth of Act 1.

- Portia's goodness and love alters him so that here he shows her the respect and honour due to her. He honestly admits to Portia that **'you shall see how much I was a braggart'**.

- He freely tells her that he was a show-off who presented a facade of wealth to impress her.

> "In such a night/ Troilus methinks mounted the Troyan walls"

• Newly-weds Lorenzo and Jessica talk of the moonlit night, comparing it nights in which famous lovers met.

• Shakespeare uses the moonlit night as a traditional **setting** for the lovers in Act Five, reinforcing the importance of love in the finale of the play.

Context: The ideal of courtly love was revived in the Elizabethan era. It was the idealistic and noble admiration of lovers for each other and often referred to Greek mythology. Lorenzo and Jessica's conversation represent this literary tradition, and show the pure and uplifting nature of love.

Grade 9 Exploration:
Look at the theme in a different way

Is the play a celebration of love?

Yes: The play concludes with all three lovers united under the moonlit sky, their relationships cemented in the institution of marriage. Love is seen as the emotion which crosses racial and religious divides; Jessica says of her engagement **'I shall end this strife/ Become a Christian and thy loving wife'**, showing how romance and commitment can heal conflict. Furthermore, the casket task reveals the genuine nature of love; love is true and deep, not based on artificial appearances, and Bassanio sees this when he says **'thou gaudy gold/Hard food for Midas, I will none of thee'** and chooses the dull lead casket and so secures Portia.

No: The relationships do not necessarily celebrate love. Love is seen as fickle as Gratiano states that he enjoys the thrill of the chase more than committed relationships, that women **'are with more spirit chased than enjoy'd'**; this does not bode well for his relationship with Nerissa. Similarly, there are possible cracks in Jessica and Lorenzo's marriage already appearing; her last words of the play are **'I am never merry when I hear sweet music'** suggesting that, far from being a joyous bride, she is already melancholy. Even Portia and Bassanio's love can be viewed as a relationship based on a monetary transaction and physical appearance.

Shakespeare followed the classic five act structure that was used in Greek theatre where the ending brings resolution. 'The Merchant of Venice' fits the tradition of Shakespeare's other plays such as 'Much Ado About Nothing' and 'A Midsummer's Night's Dream' where the couples all end up happily united.

Shakespeare uses the moonlit night at the end as a traditional *setting* for lovers, reinforcing the importance of love in the finale of the play.

Love is seen as passionate and joyful as Jessica and Lorenzo are united. It is able to transcend the race boundaries that divide Venetian society.

'in such a night
Troilus methinks mounted the Troyan walls'

'Lorenzo, certain, and my love indeed'

Love is a central theme.

Love is powerful.

Love

Love changes the characters.

Is the play a celebration of love?

'This house, these servants and this same myself/
Are yours, my lord: I give them with this ring'

Yes: Love is true and deep and Bassanio acknowledges this when he chooses the dull lead casket.

Portia gives up her independence for love; the *list* shows how entirely she submits to her love.

No: Love does not bring happinesss; for example, Jessica says **'I am never merry when I hear sweet music'** suggesting that, far from being a joyous bride, she is already melancholy.

Sample GCSE Exam Question

Read the following extract from Act 3 Scene 2.
Answer both questions below the text.
*At this point in the play, Bassanio has chosen the lead casket
and he and Portia are sealing their engagement.*

PORTIA
Myself and what is mine to you and yours
Is now converted: but now I was the lord
Of this fair mansion, master of my servants,
Queen o'er myself: and even now, but now,
This house, these servants and this same myself
Are yours, my lord: I give them with this ring;
Which when you part from, lose, or give away,
Let it presage the ruin of your love
And be my vantage to exclaim on you.
BASSANIO
Madam, you have bereft me of all words,
Only my blood speaks to you in my veins;
And there is such confusion in my powers,
As after some oration fairly spoke
By a beloved prince, there doth appear
Among the buzzing pleased multitude;
Where every something, being blent together,
Turns to a wild of nothing, save of joy,
Express'd and not express'd. But when this ring
Parts from this finger, then parts life from hence:

O, then be bold to say Bassanio's dead!
NERISSA
My lord and lady, it is now our time,
That have stood by and seen our wishes prosper,
To cry, good joy: good joy, my lord and lady!
GRATIANO
My lord Bassanio and my gentle lady,
I wish you all the joy that you can wish;
For I am sure you can wish none from me:
And when your honours mean to solemnize
The bargain of your faith, I do beseech you,
Even at that time I may be married too.
BASSANIO
With all my heart, so thou canst get a wife.
GRATIANO
I thank your lordship, you have got me one.
My eyes, my lord, can look as swift as yours:
You saw the mistress, I beheld the maid;
You loved, I loved for intermission.
No more pertains to me, my lord, than you.

a) Write about how love is presented in this extract.

b) Write about how love is presented in the play as a whole.

Sample GCSE Answer

☑ Start with the point that love is presented as a genuine emotion

This scene cements the love of Bassanio and Portia as Bassanio chooses the right casket and therefore wins Portia. Earlier in the play, Nerissa talks of how the casket task had been designed by Portia's father to ensure that only a man who truly loves her will be able to choose the right casket, that she will **'never be chosen by any rightly but one who shall rightly love'**. The audience sees paternal love here as, from the grave, Portia's father tries to protect his daughter from an unhappy marriage. Her father was clearly aware of the deceptive nature of love and how the lines between appearance and reality can be blurred. Bassanio's successful completion of the task proves that he is the correct partner for Portia, and his delight is evident as he says **'madam, you have bereft me of all words/ Only my blood speaks to you in my veins'**. The *metaphor* shows how natural and passionate his love is; his whole body is reacting to Portia's declaration of love, reinforcing the idea that their love is deep and true, and that there is a fundamental connection between them that means that they communicate on a raw, physical level.

✓ Move to the point that love brings great happiness

This true love is seen as something to celebrate in the play. Nerissa joins in the celebrations as she calls out **'good joy: good joy, my lord and lady!'** The *repetition* of **'good joy'** and the *exclamatory sentence* reinforces that the union of Bassanio and Portia is something to rejoice in. This happiness that love brings is seen earlier when Jessica checks that it is Lorenzo who is come, disguised in a mask, to take her from Shylock's house, and says **'Lorenzo, certain, and my love indeed'**. The use of **'certain'** and **'indeed'** captures Jessica's relief and joy, and their utter commitment, as she is united with Lorenzo and leaves her home to be his bride. The delight in love is also reaffirmed in Act Five; newly-weds Lorenzo and Jessica talk of the moonlit night, comparing it to nights in which famous lovers met, such as **'in such a night/ Troilus methinks mounted the Troyan walls'**. The ideal of courtly love was revived in the Elizabethan era. It was the idealistic and noble admiration of lovers for each other and often referred to Greek mythology. Lorenzo and Jessica's conversation represent this literary tradition, and show the pure and uplifting nature of love. Shakespeare also uses the moonlit night as a traditional *setting* for the lovers in Act Five, reinforcing the importance of love in the finale of the play.

✓ Make the point that love can be seen as selfless and giving

Portia gives herself entirely to Bassanio, saying **'this house, these servants and this same myself/ Are yours, my lord: I give them with this ring'**. Her love is boundless and she holds nothing back as she gives all of her possessions and herself to her betrothed. Within love, there is a submission of power and the *list* emphasises that she is giving everything; interestingly, she places herself as the last item in the *list*, implying that the material possessions are of more interest. Indeed, in the 16th century, women were the property of their husbands with no legal rights. Portia's words may seem generous and selfless yet they also reflect the stark reality of the situation as she, and and all of her property and wealth, does indeed now belong to Bassanio.

✓ Move to the point that love is used as a plot device

Love is also used as a *plot device* as the relationships between the lovers, with all the associated problems, drive the plot. This scene is the culmination of the casket task and the audience, who have watched the other suitors fail the task, will have tensely waited for Bassanio to choose the right casket, and now can sit back, relieved, as true love is celebrated. There is also a neat mirroring of Portia and Bassanio's relationship as Nerissa and Gratiano become engaged, and this mirroring is evident in Gratiano's *parallel sentence structure*: **'you saw the mistress, I beheld the maid'**. It's a satisfactory conclusion for the audience and fits the tradition of Shakespeare's other plays such as 'Much Ado About Nothing' and 'A Midsummer's Night's Dream' where the couples all end up happily united.

✓ Explore how far the play is a celebration of love

Despite the protestations of deep love in this extract, it could be argued that the relationships in the play do not necessarily celebrate love. Portia and Bassanio's love can be viewed as a relationship based on a monetary transaction and physical appearance; at the start of the play, Bassanio describes Portia as a beautiful woman whose **'sunny locks/ Hang on her temples like a golden fleece'**. The *simile* shows that he is interested in her in terms of her appearance and her wealth. The golden fleece refers to the Greek myth in which Jason and his crew of Argonauts sailed in a quest which had the golden fleece as the prize. In the 16th century, marriages were often based at least in part on financial considerations and women were expected to bring a dowry (sum of money) to their marriage, and the way that Bassanio is interested in Portia as a prize suggests that he is motivated by her wealth rather than true love. Love is also seen as fickle as Gratiano states that he enjoys the thrill of the chase more than committed relationships, that women **'are with more spirit chased than enjoy'd'**; this does not bode well for his relationship with Nerissa. Similarly, there are possible cracks in Jessica and Lorenzo's marriage already appearing by Act Five; her last words of the play are **'I am never merry when I hear sweet music'**, suggesting that, far from being a joyous bride, she is already melancholy. Depending on the production and the director's choices, these more negative views of love could be emphasised and so undermine the idea of the pure, true love we might see on the surface.

Prejudice is firmly rooted in all of the characters. Shakespeare explores how prejudice acts as a motivator and how it can generate deadly hatred.

"I hate him for he is a Christian"

- Shylock states that he hates Antonio because of Antonio's religion.

- The stark **declarative statement** leaves the audience in no doubt about the depth of Shylock's hatred. The reason for this hatred is evident in the sentence construction; the **conjunction 'for'** links the two **clauses** together and shows how the hatred is inextricably linked to religion.

Context: Shakespeare's audience would not have been familiar with Jews as Jews had been expelled from England in 1290. However, Christopher Marlowe's play, 'The Jew of Malta', performed in 1592, also portrays a money-obsessed, revenge-seeking Jew named Barabas; Shakespeare's portrayal of Shylock is similar to Marlowe's and reinforced Elizabethan prejudiced perceptions of Jews.

"You call me misbeliever, cut-throat dog/ And spit upon my Jewish gaberdine"

- Shylock reminds Antonio about how he has been appallingly treated by him.

- Antonio has abused Shylock, calling him a **'cut-throat dog'**. By reducing Shylock to the status of an animal, the audience is aware that Shylock is dehumanised.

- Antonio has also physically abused Shylock by spitting on his cloak. This shows the complete contempt Antonio has for Shylock. The way that Shylock emphasises his **'Jewish gaberdine'** shows that he believes he is being abused because of his race.

Context: Christianity was a cornerstone of society in Elizabethan England. Antonio's lack of religious tolerance would not be as shocking for Shakespeare's audience as it is for a modern audience.

> **"most vilely in the afternoon, when he is drunk"**

- Portia states that she dislikes the Duke of Saxony's nephew when he is drunk.

- Portia refers to national stereotypes when she lists her suitors and here refers to the contemporary perception that the Germans were heavy drinkers. Prejudice is engrained in all of the characters.

Context: Laughing at national stereotypes was acceptable in Elizabethan England and Portia's humorous dismissal of her multinational suitors would have been entertaining for Shakespeare's audience.

> **"He lends out money gratis and brings down/ The rate of usance here with us in Venice"**

- Shylock states that one of the reasons for his hatred for Antonio is the way that Antonio lends money without interest, undermining his own business.

- Prejudice is seen as a cause for conflict and also drives the plot. There is resentment between Antonio and Shylock because of the financial regulations (see context box).

Context: Venice's laws were divisive as only Jews were allowed to charge interest on loaned money. Prejudice was cemented in the society through the unequal laws.

> "But though I am a daughter to his blood, I am not to his manners"

- Jessica rejects her father as she states that she might have been born Jewish but her personality is different to her father's.

- There is hope here for love to transcend (overcome) prejudice as Jessica and Lorenzo fall in love despite the racial divide.

Context: Jewish descent is traced through the females in the Jewish family. For Jessica to marry outside her religion and convert to Christianity would have been a disaster for Shylock as it would mean the end of his bloodline.

Grade 9 Exploration:
Look at the theme in a different way

Does Shakespeare use the play to bolster (strengthen) or to challenge Jewish stereotypes?

Bolster: There seems little doubt that Shakespeare plays on contemporary stereotypes of Jews and so shows an innate prejudice. Shylock is resistant to integration as he is reluctant to dine with the Christians and he openly shows his horror as his daughter marries a Christian. More pertinently, in the courtroom scene, the audience graphically sees Shylock intent on bloody revenge sharpening his knife to slice Antonio open and refusing to back down. He *repeatedly* refuses to show mercy, and indeed mercy is portrayed as a Christian quality coming from God; Portia describes mercy as **'it droppeth as the gentle rain from heaven'**. The *contrast* of this beautiful *simile* to Shylock's obsessive, determined **'I will have my bond'** shows the audience that Jews are bloodthirsty and vicious and the Christians are the keepers of mercy and goodness.

Challenge: One of the most powerful lines from the play is Shylock's passionate appeal to the Christians as he demands of Salerino **'if you prick us, do we not bleed?'** The *rhetorical question* emphasises the humanity of the Jewish race. Shylock forces the characters, and the audience, to acknowledge that the Jews are not inhuman; they are people who behave in exactly the same way as the Christians. Perhaps one of Shakespeare's purposes in writing the play was to show how religious intolerances are destructive and how it is humanity, not race or religion, which is important.

The **conjunction 'for'** links the two **clauses** together and shows how Shylock's hatred is inextricably linked to religion.

Portia mocks her German suitor, playing on national stereotypes.

'I hate him for he is a Christian'

'most vilely in the afternoon, when he is drunk'

Prejudice is based on religion and race.

Prejudice is universal.

Prejudice & Hate

Prejudice causes conflict and drives the plot.

Does Shakespeare bolster or challenge Jewish stereotypes?

'He lends out money gratis and brings down/ The rate of usance here with us in Venice'

Bolster: the audience sees the Jewish Shylock viciously intent on bloody revenge while mercy is presented as a Christian quality.

There is resentment between Antonio and Shylock because of the unbalanced financial regulations based on prejudice; this fuels the plot.

Challenge: Shylock forces the audience to see Jews as humans, not animals, as he demands, **'if you prick us, do we not bleed?'**

Read the following extract from Act 1 Scene 3.
Answer both questions below the text.

At this point in the play, Shylock has just finished telling a Biblical story to Antonio as part of a discussion about money-lending. The story is from the Old Testament and Shylock recounts how Jacob tricked Laban to make his flock of sheep more profitable.

ANTONIO
This was a venture, sir, that Jacob served for;
A thing not in his power to bring to pass,
But sway'd and fashion'd by the hand of heaven.
Was this inserted to make interest good?
Or is your gold and silver ewes and rams?
SHYLOCK
I cannot tell; I make it breed as fast:
But note me, signior.
ANTONIO
Mark you this, Bassanio,
The devil can cite Scripture for his purpose.
An evil soul producing holy witness
Is like a villain with a smiling cheek,
A goodly apple rotten at the heart:
O, what a goodly outside falsehood hath!

SHYLOCK
Three thousand ducats; 'tis a good round sum.
Three months from twelve; then, let me see; the
rate—
ANTONIO
Well, Shylock, shall we be beholding to you?
SHYLOCK
Signior Antonio, many a time and oft
In the Rialto you have rated me
About my moneys and my usances:
Still have I borne it with a patient shrug,
For sufferance is the badge of all our tribe.
You call me misbeliever, cut-throat dog,
And spit upon my Jewish gaberdine,
And all for use of that which is mine own.

a) How are ideas about prejudice presented in this extract?

b) How are ideas about prejudice presented in the play?

Sample GCSE Answer

 Start with the point that prejudice is central to the plot

Prejudice is central to the plot. The tension and dislike between Antonio and Shylock drives the plot of the **'pound of flesh'**, and here Shakespeare shows us how prejudice forms the source of the men's mutual hatred. Shylock reminds Antonio how he has **'rated me/About my moneys and my usances'**. Venice's laws were divisive as only Jews were allowed to charge interest on loaned money and there is deep resentment between Antonio and Shylock because of these financial regulations. Shylock refers to the money he makes, saying that **'I make it (his gold) breed as fast'**. There might well be jealousy and resentment on Antonio's part that he is not allowed to make money in the way that Shylock can; prejudice is cemented in Venice's society through the unequal laws.

 Move to the point that the Christians show prejudice towards the Jewish Shylock

This embedded prejudice that Shylock suffers from being a Jew is evident in his bitter account of how Antonio has treated him in an appalling manner: **'you call me misbeliever, cut-throat dog, And spit upon my Jewish**

gaberdine'. By reducing Shylock to the status of an animal, the audience is aware that Shylock is dehumanised. Antonio has also physically abused Shylock by spitting on his cloak and this shows the complete contempt Antonio has for Shylock. The way that Shylock emphasises how his **'Jewish gaberdine'** is spat upon shows that he believes he is being abused because of his race and religion. Christianity was a cornerstone of society in Elizabethan England and Antonio's lack of religious tolerance would not be as shocking for Shakespeare's audience as it is for a modern audience. This prejudice is not just shown by Antonio; elsewhere in the novel, Shylock is addressed by the other characters as **'Jew'** as they constantly define him by his race.

✔ Move to the point that Shylock shows prejudice towards the Christians

Yet the prejudice is mutual; Shylock speaks of how **'sufferance is the badge of all our tribe'**, referring to how the Jewish people have been persistently persecuted. He uses the ***noun* 'tribe'** to reflect the tight-knit community of the Jews and to illustrate the racial divide between Shylock and the Christians. Shylock seems to take pride in this separation through his use of the ***possessive pronoun* 'our'**. He has no wish to mingle with the Christians and sets himself out as different; his acceptance of the abuse with a passive, meek **'patient shrug'** sharply ***contrasts*** with the ***list*** of Antonio's active, violent abuse. Yet this acceptance is perhaps only superficial as his own hatred runs deep. Earlier in the scene, Shylock states that he hates Antonio because of Antonio's religion, saying **'I hate him for he is a Christian'**. The stark ***declarative statement*** leaves the audience in no doubt about the depth of Shylock's hatred. The reason for this hatred is evident in the sentence construction; the ***conjunction* 'for'** links the two clauses together and shows how the hatred is inextricably linked to religion.

✔ Explore the point that prejudice is completely ingrained in the play's characters

In this scene, the prejudice is vicious and corrosive as Shylock begins to plant the seeds of his grisly revenge. Yet the prejudice is so entrenched in the play's characters that Shakespeare uses it for comic purposes as well. Portia refers to national stereotypes when she ***lists*** her suitors and refers to the contemporary perception that the Germans were heavy drinkers, dismissing the Duke of Saxony's nephew's behaviour as **'most vilely in the afternoon, when he is drunk'**. Laughing at national stereotypes was acceptable in Elizabethan England and Portia's humorous dismissal of her multinational suitors would have been entertaining for Shakespeare's audience.

✔ Explore how far Shakespeare uses the play to bolster or challenge stereotypes

There seems little doubt that Shakespeare plays on contemporary stereotypes of Jews and so shows an innate prejudice in his depiction of Shylock. Shakespeare's audience would not have been familiar with Jews as Jews had been expelled from England in 1290. Shylock is resistant to integration as he is reluctant to dine with the Christians and openly shows his horror as his daughter marries a Christian. More pertinently, in the courtroom scene, the audience graphically sees Shylock intent on bloody revenge sharpening his knife to slice Antonio open and refusing to back down. He ***repeatedly*** refuses to show mercy, and mercy is portrayed as an essentially Christian quality; Portia describes mercy as **'it droppeth as the gentle rain from heaven'**. The contrast of this beautiful ***simile*** to Shylock's obsessive, determined **'I will have my bond'** shows the audience that Jews are bloodthirsty and vicious and the Christians are the keepers of mercy and goodness. Christopher Marlowe's play, 'The Jew of Malta', performed in1592, also portrays a money-obsessed, revenge-seeking Jew named Barabas; Shakespeare's portrayal of Shylock is similar to Marlowe's and reinforced Elizabethan perceptions of Jews. Yet despite this, there is a strong argument that Shakespeare creates and uses the character of Shylock to highlight and condemn prejudice. Few audiences can forget one of the most powerful lines from the play as Shylock passionately demands of Salerino: **'if you prick us, do we not bleed?'** The ***rhetorical question*** emphasises the humanity of the Jewish race. Shylock forces the characters, and the audience, to see that the Jews are not inhuman; they are people who behave in exactly the same way as the Christians. Perhaps one of Shakespeare's purposes in writing the play was to show how religious intolerances are destructive and how it is humanity, not race or religion, which is important.

10 Friendship
Exploration of a theme

Friendship is a central theme to the play with the bonds of friendships between the characters driving the plot.

> "My purse, my person, my extremest means, Lie all unlock'd to your occasions"

- Antonio promises his dear friend, Bassanio, to help him financially.

- The **list** shows how the men's friendship is deep and generous. The **repetition** of the **personal possessive pronoun 'my'** emphasises how giving Antonio is; he holds nothing back in his desire to help his friend.

> "You shall not seal to such a bond for me"

- Bassanio initially refuses to allow Antonio to accept Shylock's terms of the loan.

- He too seems to value his friendship and does not want to place Antonio in any danger.

- Yet, very quickly, Antonio does seal the bond and Bassanio does not really protest again. It would seem that Bassanio is willing to let Antonio risk everything to help him acquire the wealth he seeks. The audience might well question whether this relationship is an unequal one and whether Bassanio is manipulating the friendship to suit his own ends.

"All my fortunes are at sea' 'dangerous rocks...enrobe the roaring waters with my silks"

- Antonio admits that he has no spare money as he waits for his merchant ships to return to Venice through the perilous seas. Antonio's love for his friend places him in danger and therefore drives the plot.

- There are many references to the treacherous nature of the boats' journeys in the play; the **metaphor 'enrobe the roaring waters with my silks'** graphically illustrates how cargo can be lost.

Context: Shakespeare's audience were aware of the perilous nature of sea journeys and so a sense of unease is created as Antonio pledges to return money which he does not yet have for the sake of his friendship.

"I think he only loves the world for him"

- Solanio says that Antonio has an incredibly deep love for Bassanio.

- The men's friendship is clearly an intense one. The **adverb 'only'** shows the exclusivity of this friendship, and the audience sees the depth of the emotion that Antonio feels.

Context: An audience might wonder whether this friendship has its basis in homosexual love yet male friendships in Elizabethan society were often emotionally intense.

"I thank thee, good Tubal: good news!/ 'Thou stickest a dagger in me"

- After Jessica's elopement, Shylock reacts to his friend Tubal's reports which alternate between good news about Antonio's financial losses and bad news about Jessica's behaviour in Genoa. Shylock does take comfort from his friend.

- Arguably, Tubal's deliberate **juxtaposition** of the good and bad news riles Shylock, increasing his emotional pain and fuelling his disastrous desire for revenge. This is not the action of a good friend.

Context: In Venice, the Jewish community were forced to live by law in a segregated part of the city called a ghetto. This limited their chances of forming relationships with anyone outside their community; the friendship of Tubal and Shylock might be based on circumstance rather than genuine camaraderie.

> "Superfluity comes sooner by white hairs, but competency lives longer"

- Nerissa gives Portia sensible advice, reminding her that excess living ages us and that to have just enough money means a longer, healthier life.

- The relationship between the two women is warm and close, full of laughter and fun. Nerissa is devoted to Portia and seeks to comfort and advise her.

Context: Shakespeare's plays often celebrate the relationships between women, such as Hero and Beatrice in 'Much Ado About Nothing' or Helena and Hermia is 'A Midsummer Night's Dream'.

Grade 9 Exploration:
Look at the theme in a different way

Is the play a celebration of friendship?

Yes: The play celebrates the strong bonds of friendships that bind the characters. An example of this is during the court scene when the intense drama is ramped up as Bassanio offers himself to save Antonio, saying **'the Jew shall have my flesh, blood, bones and all'**. The *list* captures how wholeheartedly Bassanio gives himself up for his friend, each item dramatically giving every part of his body and culminating in the word **'all'** to illustrate the depth of his friendship. The *modal verb* **'shall'** reflects his absolute determination to help his beloved friend at the cost of his own life, illustrating how the power of friendship has positively changed the superificial, ambitious young man that we saw at the beginning of the play. Indeed, there is an echo of the *list structure* that Antonio uses in Act 1 when he tells Bassanio **'my purse, my person, my extremest means, Lie all unlock'd to your occasions'**, reflecting how Bassanio has learnt lessons and realigned his values so that he understands and returns the great friendship that Antonio has shown him.

No: Bassanio plays on his friendship with Antonio for his own personal gain, and his dramatic offer in the courtroom to die for Antonio is a showy one lacking in substance; he only suggests this as he knows that the law will not allow it. The language that both he and Antonio use has echoes of a commercial transaction; for example, Bassanio tells his friend that it is to him that **'I owe the most in money and in love, And from your love I have a warranty'**. This language of business and trade suggests that the characters view friendship in terms of loss and gain rather than something natural and loving. Furthermore, the friendships are all unequal: for example, Portia and Nerissa's cheerful friendship is undermined by their relative positions of mistress and servant, with the in-built inequality that this difference in social situation would bring. It could therefore be argued that the friendships within the play are functional and cold rather than deep and lasting.

The **adverb 'only'** shows the exclusivity of Antonio and Bassanio's friendship, and the audience sees the depth of the emotion that Antonio feels.

The **repetition** of the **personal possessive pronoun 'my'** emphasises how giving Antonio is; he holds nothing back in his desire to help his friend.

'I think he only loves the world for him'

'My purse, my person, my extremest means, Lie all unlock'd to your occasions'

Friendships can be intense.

Friendships can be generous.

Friendship

Friendships drive the plot.

Is the play a celebration of friendship?

'all my fortunes are at sea' 'dangerous rocks... enrobe the roaring waters with my silks'

Yes: The bonds of friendship are clearly shown when Bassanio offers himself to save Antonio, saying **'The Jew shall have my flesh, blood, bones and all'**.

Antonio's love for his friend places him in danger and therefore adds **dramatic tension**.

No: The friendships are unequal and shallow, limited by social status and viewed in terms of personal gain.

Read the following extract from Act 3 Scene 2.
Answer both questions below the text.

At this point in the play, Bassanio has just received news that Antonio is in deep trouble over the failure to repay Shylock's loan.

PORTIA
Is it your dear friend that is thus in trouble?
BASSANIO
The dearest friend to me, the kindest man,
The best-condition'd and unwearied spirit
In doing courtesies, and one in whom
The ancient Roman honour more appears
Than any that draws breath in Italy.
PORTIA
What sum owes he the Jew?
BASSANIO
For me three thousand ducats.
PORTIA
What, no more?
Pay him six thousand, and deface the bond;
Double six thousand, and then treble that,
Before a friend of this description
Shall lose a hair through Bassanio's fault.
First go with me to church and call me wife,
And then away to Venice to your friend;
For never shall you lie by Portia's side

With an unquiet soul. You shall have gold
To pay the petty debt twenty times over:
When it is paid, bring your true friend along.
My maid Nerissa and myself meantime
Will live as maids and widows. Come, away!
For you shall hence upon your wedding-day:
Bid your friends welcome, show a merry cheer:
Since you are dear bought, I will love you dear.
But let me hear the letter of your friend.
BASSANIO
[Reads] Sweet Bassanio, my ships have all
miscarried, my creditors grow cruel, my estate is
very low, my bond to the Jew is forfeit; and since
in paying it, it is impossible I should live, all
debts are cleared between you and I, if I might but
see you at my death. Notwithstanding, use your
pleasure: if your love do not persuade you to come,
let not my letter.
PORTIA
O love, dispatch all business, and be gone!

a) Discuss how friendships are presented in this extract.

b) Discuss how friendships are presented in the play as a whole.

☑ Start with the point that friendship is central to the plot

This extract marks the build-up to the climax of the play. In the midst of the joy of his betrothal, Bassanio receives news that his friend is in trouble. Knowing the deep friendship between the two men, the audience empathises with the emotional turmoil of Bassanio, wondering how he will respond. The **contrast** between Bassanio's happiness at wining Portia's hand and then his anguish creates **dramatic tension**. Elsewhere in the play, this use of friendship as a **plot device** is also evident. In Act One, Antonio admits that he has no spare money as he waits for his merchant ships to return to Venice, saying **'all my fortunes are at sea'** and **'dangerous rocks…enrobe the roaring waters with my silks'**. The **metaphor** 'enrobe the roaring waters with my silks' graphically shows how cargo can be lost while the **adjectives** 'dangerous' and 'roaring' emphasise the vicious nature of the sea which can easily destroy the fragile boats and their cargo; indeed, at this point of the play, his ships **'have all miscarried'**. Venice was one of the great trading ports of Europe and Shakespeare's audience was aware of its reputation as a place where enormous wealth was generated. Yet they were also aware of the perilous nature of sea journeys and so a sense of unease is created from the beginning as Antonio pledges to return money which he does not yet have for the sake of his friendship. Antonio's love for his friend places him in danger and therefore drives the plot until the inevitable happens and, as Antonio's letter admits in the extract, that **'my ships have all miscarried'**.

✓ Move to the point that friendship is seen as very important

Friendship is presented as so important that it transcends (overcomes) marital relationships. Despite it being his wedding day, Bassanio is desperate to leave and help his friend, and Portia endorses this, urging him **'o love, dispatch all business, and be gone!'** The *imperative verb* 'dispatch' and the *exclamatory sentence* reflects the genuine understanding that Portia has that friendship is of the utmost value. Later in the play, we see this acceptance by other characters that friendship is placed above love as Gratanio wishes Nerissa dead if it could prevent Antonio's suffering.

✓ Move to the point that friendships are intense

Friendships are emotionally intense. In the extract, Bassanio describes his friend as **'the dearest friend to me, the kindest man/The best-condition'd and unwearied spirit'**. The triplet of *superlatives* 'dearest' 'kindest' 'best' reflects how passionately Bassanio feels about his friend and Antonio reciprocates this passion in his letter as he writes **'if I might but see you at my death'**. The *conditional phrase* here reflects Antonio's longing to see Bassanio one more time. The depth of the men's friendship has been apparent from the beginning of the play; Solanio says that Antonio has an incredibly deep love for Bassanio, claiming that **'I think he only loves the world for him'**. The *adverb* 'only' captures the exclusivity of this friendship, and the strong emotions that Antonio feels. An audience might wonder whether this friendship has its basis in homosexual love yet male friendships in Elizabethan society were often emotionally intense.

✓ Start exploring how far the play is a celebration of friendship

The play celebrates the strong bonds of friendships that bind the characters. At the start, Nerissa gives Portia sensible advice, reminding her that excess living ages us and that to have just enough money means a longer, healthier life. The relationship between the two women is warm and close, and full of laughter and fun and, indeed, Shakespeare's plays often celebrate the relationships between women, such as Hero and Beatrice in 'Much Ado About Nothing'. Other friendships are presented positively; an example of this in during the court scene when the intense drama is ramped up as Bassanio offers to die himself to save Antonio, saying **'the Jew shall have my flesh, blood, bones and all'**. The *list* captures how wholeheartedly Bassanio gives himself up for his friend, each item dramatically giving every part of his body and culminating in the word **'all'** to illustrate the depth of his friendship. The *modal verb* 'shall' reflects his absolute determination to help his beloved friend at the cost of his own life, illustrating how the power of friendship has positively changed the superificial, ambitious young man that we saw at the beginning of the play. Indeed, there is an echo of the *list structure* that Antonio uses in Act 1 when he tells Bassanio **'my purse, my person, my extremest means, Lie all unlock'd to your occasions'**, reflecting how Bassanio has learnt lessons and realigned his values so that he now understands and returns the great friendship that Antonio has shown him.

✓ Develop this exploration of how far the play is a celebration of friendship

Yet an audience might well question the authenticity of the friendships in the play. For example, Bassanio plays on his friendship with Antonio for his own personal gain, and his dramatic offer in the courtroom to die for Antonio is a showy one lacking in substance; he only suggests this as he knows that the law will not allow it. The language that both he and Antonio use has echoes of a commercial transaction; for example, Bassanio tells his friend that it is to him that **'I owe the most in money and in love, And from your love I have a warranty'**. This language of business and trade suggests that the characters view friendship in terms of loss and gain rather than something natural and loving. Furthermore, the friendships are all unequal: for example, Portia and Nerissa's friendship is that of mistress and servant and Portia reminds us of that in the extract as she says **'my maid Nerissa and myself'**. Their cheerful friendship is undermined by their relative positions of mistress and servant, with the in-built inequality that this difference in social situation would bring. It could therefore be argued that the friendships are functional and cold rather than deep and lasting. There are many aspects to the friendships in the play, yet this is true of real life; few friendships are entirely straightforward.

The desire for revenge is the emotion that drives the plot between Shylock and Antonio. Shylock shows no mercy but in turn is given none, and the question of whether anyone receives justice at the end of the play is left open to interpretation.

"I will feed fat the ancient grudge I bear him"

• Shylock clearly states that he plans revenge on Antonio.

• He relishes the thought of revenge. The **metaphor** of Shylock feasting on Antonio's suffering is a chilling one and this sinister image is enhanced by the soft **alliteration** of **'feed fat'** which creates a sense of unsavoury enjoyment.

"You call me misbeliever, cut-throat dog, / And spit upon my Jewish gaberdine"

• Shylock reminds Antonio about how he has been appallingly treated by him.

• Antonio has abused Shylock, calling him a **'cut-throat dog'**. By reducing Shylock to the status of an animal, the audience is aware that Shylock is dehumanised. We understand that Shylock has valid reasons for seeking revenge on one who has openly attacked him.

Context: Christianity was a cornerstone of society in Elizabethan England. Antonio's lack of religious tolerance would not be as shocking for Shakespeare's audience as it is for a modern audience. Yet maybe all audiences would wonder whether there is any justice at the end, when Antonio is never brought to account for his dreadful treatment of Shylock.

"The duke cannot deny the course of the law"

- Antonio states that Shylock is entitled to his gruesome bond by law and no one, not even the duke, can stop him.

- The law is the instrument that delivers justice in Venice. Regardless of any morality, the law brings Antonio to the brink of death.

Context: Venice was one of the great trading ports of Europe and its laws protected the trade and wealth that its citizens enjoyed. The Duke is unable to override this law to help Antonio in case it undermined the vital trade.

"Tarry a little; there is something else. / This bond doth give thee here no jot of blood"

- Portia stops Shylock from killing Antonio by using Venice's laws.

- This is a moment of intense *dramatic tension* as Portia halts Shylock's knife with her command '**tarry a little**'.

- She uses the strict terms of the law to save Antonio; Shylock can take the flesh but not the blood and so Shylock is deprived of his revenge.

> **"Portia, forgive me this enforced wrong"**

- Bassanio begs Portia to forgive him for giving away the ring.
- There is humour here for the audience and this humour reinforces the theme of forgiveness and mercy.
- Shakespeare perhaps uses the play to show us that it is wrong to seek revenge and much better to show mercy.

Context: Shakespeare uses the classic five act structure from Greek theatre to emphasise ideas of compassion. At the end of the play which marks the *resolution* of the conflict, all is forgiven and the characters are reconciled in a moonlit atmosphere of peace and harmony after the high drama of the courtroom.

Grade 9 Exploration:
Look at the theme in a different way

Does Shakespeare present mercy as a Christian quality?

Yes: In the courtroom scene, the audience graphically sees Shylock intent on bloody revenge, sharpening his knife to slice Antonio open and refusing to back down. He *repeatedly* refuses to show mercy and indeed, mercy is portrayed as a Christian quality; Portia describes mercy as **'it droppeth as the gentle rain from heaven'**. The *contrast* of this beautiful *simile* to Shylock's obsessive, determined **'I will have my bond'** ensures that Shakespeare presents Jews as cold and merciless compared to the charitable Christians.

No: Portia ruthlessly traps Shylock. She, and the other Christians, show no mercy to Shylock, who loses everything: his wealth, his family, even his religion. At the end, he is isolated, humiliated and silenced, and there is huge *pathos* (pity) as he utters his last words of the play: **'I pray you, give me leave to go from hence; I am not well'**. If this is justice for Shylock's ruthless revenge, then it is perhaps excessive. And indeed, Shylock openly exposes the Christians' lack of mercy and compassion when he accuses them of using their slaves in **'abject and in slavish parts'**. No mercy is shown by the Christians for their wretched slaves; it seems that it is humankind in general that lacks compassion rather than mercy being the province of any religion.

The slave trade had begun in Elizabethan England when John Hawkyns sailed on direct orders from Queen Elizabeth to capture humans. It was a relatively new trade to Shakespeare's audience, and Shakespeare might well have been asking the audience to question the morality of slavery, with its complete lack of mercy, through Shylock's words.

He seems to relish the thought of revenge. The *metaphor* of Shylock feasting on Antonio's suffering is a chilling one.

The law is the instrument that delivers justice in Venice.
Regardless of any morality, the law brings Antonio to the brink of death.

'I will feed fat the ancient grudge I bear him'

'The duke cannot deny the course of the law'

Revenge motivates Shylock.

The law is viewed as paramount (important).

Revenge & Justice

Mercy is seen as important.

Does Shakespeare show mercy as a Christian quality?

'Portia, forgive me this enforced wrong'

Yes: the audience sees Shylock viciously intent on bloody revenge while mercy is presented as a Christian quality.

The humour of Bassanio begging for forgiveness for the ring debacle reinforces the theme of forgiveness and mercy.

No: Portia ruthlessly traps Shylock. She, and the other Christians, show no mercy to Shylock, who loses everything: his wealth, his family, even his religion.

Read the following extract from Act 4 Scene 1.
Answer both questions below the text.
At this point in the play, the Duke and Bassanio are trying to persuade Shylock to show mercy to Antonio.

ANTONIO
I pray you, think you question with the Jew:
You may as well go stand upon the beach
And bid the main flood bate his usual height;
You may as well use question with the wolf
Why he hath made the ewe bleat for the lamb;
You may as well forbid the mountain pines
To wag their high tops and to make no noise,
When they are fretten with the gusts of heaven;
You may as well do anything most hard,
As seek to soften that–than which what's harder?–
His Jewish heart: therefore, I do beseech you,
Make no more offers, use no farther means,
But with all brief and plain conveniency
Let me have judgment and the Jew his will.
BASSANIO
For thy three thousand ducats here is six.
SHYLOCK
What judgment shall I dread, doing
Were in six parts and every part a ducat,
I would not draw them; I would have my bond.
DUKE
How shalt thou hope for mercy, rendering none?
SHYLOCK
What judgment shall I dread, doing no wrong?
You have among you many a purchased slave,
Which, like your asses and your dogs and mules,
You use in abject and in slavish parts,
Because you bought them: shall I say to you,
Let them be free, marry them to your heirs?
Why sweat they under burthens? let their beds
Be made as soft as yours and let their palates
Be season'd with such viands? You will answer
'The slaves are ours:' so do I answer you:
The pound of flesh, which I demand of him,
Is dearly bought; 'tis mine and I will have it.
If you deny me, fie upon your law!
There is no force in the decrees of Venice.
I stand for judgment: answer; shall I have it?

a) How are ideas of revenge and mercy explored in this extract?
b) How are ideas of revenge and mercy explored in the play as a whole?

 Start with the point that Shylock is intent on revenge

In this extract, we see how Shylock is obsessed with revenge. It is clear that he desires Antonio's death as he dismisses Bassanio's offer to double the value of the bond. Shylock's **hyperbolic** language shows that he would not waive the penalty even if Bassonio's offer were increased six-fold: **'were in six parts and every part a ducat'**. He is not interested in repayment of the loan with interest, which would be more than fair; he is bent on revenge. This desire for revenge is clear from the opening act when Shylock clearly states that **'I will feed fat the ancient grudge I bear him'**, relishing the thought of revenge. The **metaphor** of Shylock feasting on Antonio's suffering is a chilling one and this sinister **image** is enhanced by the soft **alliteration** of **'feed fat'** which creates a sense of unsavoury enjoyment.

 Move to the point that Shylock sees his revenge on Antonio as just

Shylock views his revenge as justice for the treatment he has received from Antonio because of his religion and race. Certainly, in the courtroom scene, he is **repeatedly** referred to as an outsider- **'the Jew'**- and is therefore isolated and despised. Earlier in the play, his ill treatment is clear when Shylock reminds Antonio about how he has been appallingly treated by him, calling him **'misbeliever, cut-throat dog'** and how he has **'spit upon my Jewish gaberdine'**. By reducing Shylock to the status of an animal, the audience is aware that Shylock is dehumanised and so we understand that Shylock has valid reasons for seeking revenge on one who has openly attacked him. Christianity was a cornerstone of society in Elizabethan England and Antonio's lack of religious tolerance would not be as shocking for Shakespeare's audience as it is for a modern audience. Yet maybe all audiences wonder whether there is any justice at the end, when Antonio is never brought to account for his treatment on Shylock.

✔ Move to the point that the characters find Shylock's lack of mercy inhumane

Antonio describes how asking Shylock for mercy is pointless, that they might as well **'question with the wolf/ Why he hath made the ewe bleat for the lamb'**. The *metaphor* illustrates how Shylock's revenge is seen as vicious; his refusal to give mercy to the innocent lamb that is Antonio is seen as inhumane and Shylock is viewed as a **'wolf'** with its connotations of sly, ruthless violence. The Christian characters are bewildered by Shylock's intractable attitude and blame it on the fact that he is a Jew and therefore is incapable of understanding compassion and mercy. Antonio uses a *repetitive sentence structure* - **'you may as well'** -which builds on different scenarios that capture the hopelessness of asking any Jew for mercy. Certainly, Shylock does not turn away from revenge; in the courtroom scene, the audience graphically sees Shylock intent on bloody revenge, sharpening his knife to slice Antonio open and refusing to back down. He *repeatedly* refuses to show mercy and mercy is portrayed as a Christian quality; Portia describes mercy as **'it droppeth as the gentle rain from heaven'**. The *contrast* of this beautiful *simile* to Shylock's obsessive, determined **'I will have my bond'** presents Jews as bloodthirsty and vicious while the Christians are the keepers of mercy and goodness.

✔ Move to the point that very little mercy is shown in the play

Yet this is not necessarily true; arguably, none of the Christian characters display any mercy. Portia ruthlessly traps Shylock. She, and the other Christians, show no mercy to Shylock, who loses everything: his wealth, his family, even his religion. At the end he is isolated, humiliated and silenced, and there is huge *pathos* (pity) as he utters his last words of the play: **'I pray you, give me leave to go from hence; I am not well'**. If this is justice for Shylock's ruthless revenge, then it seems excessive. And indeed, Shylock openly exposes the Christians' lack of mercy and compassion when he accuses them of using their slaves in **'abject and in slavish parts'**. No mercy is shown by the Christians for their wretched slaves; it seems that it is humankind in general that lacks compassion rather than mercy being the province of any religion. Interestingly, the slave trade had begun in Elizabethan England when John Hawkyns sailed on direct orders from Queen Elizabeth to capture humans. It was a relatively new trade to Shakespeare's audience and Shakespeare might well have been asking the audience to question the morality of slavery, with its complete lack of mercy, through Shylock's words.

✔ Finish with the point that the revenge and mercy add to the dramatic tension

This is a moment of great *dramatic tension*. Shylock demands justice through the laws and reminds the Duke, **'if you deny me, fie upon your law! There is no force in the decrees of Venice.'** The law is the instrument that delivers justice in Venice and, regardless of any morality, the law brings Antonio to the brink of death. Venice was one of the great trading ports of Europe and its laws protected the trade and wealth that its citizens enjoyed. The Duke is unable to override this law to help Antonio in case it undermined this vital trade. The Duke, and the audience, see that there is no escape from the grisly bond and so the *dramatic tension* is ramped up as the characters appeal in vain to Shylock's sense of mercy. In the end, it is Portia's clever reading of the law that saves Antonio from Shylock's revenge. Yet later, in Act Five, we see how the theme of mercy is revisited in a humorous way as Bassanio begs Portia for forgiveness for giving away the ring, saying **'Portia, forgive me this enforced wrong'**. There is humour here which reinforces the theme of forgiveness and mercy. Shakespeare uses the classic five act *structure* from Greek theatre to emphasises ideas of compassion. At the end of the play which marks the *resolution* of the conflict, all is forgiven and the characters are reconciled in a moonlit atmosphere of peace and harmony after the drama of the courtroom. Shakespeare perhaps uses the play to show us that it is wrong to seek revenge and much better to show mercy.

The theme of appearance and reality weaves its way throughout the play as Shakespeare shows us that what things seem like on the surface are often not what they really are.

"A stage where every man must play a part"

- Antonio sees the world as **'a stage where every man must play a part'**.

- His **metaphor** suggests that he, and everyone else, are actors and are therefore not presenting themselves as they really are.

- His words at the start firmly establish the theme of appearance and reality.

Context: Shakespeare adapts this **metaphor** in his later plays; for example, in 'As You Like It', Jaques says **'All the world's a stage/ And all the men and women merely players'**. The repeated theatre **metaphor** reflects how Shakespeare often explores the idea of people putting forward false representations of themselves.

"The devil can cite Scripture for his purpose"

- Antonio sneers at Shylock, saying that anyone can twist the truth to suit them.

- Antonio's **analogy** shows how he despises Shylock and sees him as evil.

- There is a dark side to appearance and reality. Even though Antonio does not trust Shylock who quotes from the Bible, he still does not see through Shylock's ruse and he signs the bond. Shylock manipulates Antonio by pretending to offer friendship, tricking Antonio and taking him to the brink of death.

Context: Shakespeare's audience would not have been familiar with Jews as Jews had been expelled from England in 1290. However, Christopher Marlowe's play, 'The Jew of Malta', performed in 1592, also portrays a money-obsessed, revenge-seeking Jew named Barabas; Shakespeare's portrayal of the mercenary Shylock is similar to Marlowe's and reinforced perceptions of Jews. Antonio's comparison of Shylock to the devil reflects these attitudes.

> **"thou gaudy gold, Hard food for Midas, I will none of thee"**

- Bassanio rejects the gold casket.

- He understands that gold can dazzle and blind. The hard **alliteration** of **'gaudy gold'** captures his contempt for the showy, flashy metal. He chooses the lead casket instead, understanding that appearances can be deceptive.

- This is something which Portia's father also understood; the casket task was created in order to protect Portia from deceptive men who would trick her into an unhappy marriage.

Context: Bassanio's classical reference to the Greek myth of King Midas, whose touch turned everything to gold, reminds the audience that he is an educated man from a high-born family and worthy of Portia.

> **"Your wife would give you little thanks for that, / If she were by, to hear you make the offer"**

- Disguised as the lawyer, Portia ironically responds to Bassanio's declaration that he would rather Portia were dead if it helped Antonio.

- There is real humour here through **dramatic irony** as the audience is in on the joke; they know what Bassanio doesn't and can see the concealed Portia's indignation.

Context: Shakespeare often used disguise in his plays, drawing on the literary tradition of Greek and Roman theatre to engage and entertain the audience.

> "I have within my mind/A thousand raw tricks of these bragging Jacks"

• Portia tells Nerissa her plan to disguise herself as a man to help Antonio. Portia humorously describes how she will copy the manners of men she has seen in order to be convincing in her disguise.

• Disguise is used to visually illustrate the theme of appearance and reality. It also acts as a *plot device*, increasing *dramatic tension* as the disguised Portia travels to Venice to save doomed Antonio.

Context: In Shakespeare's original productions, the character of Portia would have been played by a boy as women were forbidden by law to be actors. The audience would have been much entertained by the comedy of the boy actor pretending to be a girl who is now pretending to be a boy.

Grade 9 Exploration:
Look at the theme in a different way

Does the play value appearance over reality?

Yes: Appearance is valued by all of the characters. All deceive each other and we see that truthful reality does not bring happiness. For example, Jessica's last words of the play are **'I am never merry when I hear sweet music'**, suggesting that, far from being a joyous bride, she is already melancholy. The audience sees that the reality of life with Lorenzo, who took her away from her father wearing a mask, is not what she expected. Bassanio chooses the lead casket, not because he is Portia's true love, but because he himself deceives, borrowing money to give himself the impression of a rich suitor. His marriage is also based on a mirage.

No: By the end of the play, appearances have been stripped away. Bassanio admits to being a **'braggart'** and tells Portia the truth about the giving away of the ring. In turn, Portia reveals the truth about the doctor and 'his' clerk. Their marriage begins positively with mutual openness and honesty.

 # Essential Exam Tip

☑ Start revising for the exams early. Revising in ten minute bursts from the end of Year 10 can make a huge difference and reduces the last minute panic before your exams.

Antonio's *metaphor* suggests that he, and everyone else, are actors and are therefore not presenting themselves as they really are.

Bassanio rejects the flashy gold casket, understanding that appearances can be deceptive.

'A stage where every man must play a part'

'thou gaudy gold, Hard food for Midas, I will none of thee'

Appearance and reality are central to the play.

Appearances are stripped away throughout the play.

Appearance & Reality

The theme of appearance and reality creates humour.

Does the play value appearance over reality?

**'Your wife would give you little thanks for that,
If she were by, to hear you make the offer'**

Yes: Appearance is valued by all of the characters. All deceive each other and we see that any attempt at truthful reality does not bring happiness.

The audience enjoys the *dramatic irony* as the disguised Portia responds to Bassanio's wish that his wife were dead.

No: By the end of the play, appearances have been stripped away. The marriages begin with open honesty.

Read the following extract from Act 3 Scene 5.
Answer both questions below the text.

At this point in the play, Portia is explaining her plan to dress herself and Nerissa up as men to save Antonio.

NERISSA
Shall they see us?
PORTIA
They shall, Nerissa; but in such a habit,
That they shall think we are accomplished
With that we lack. I'll hold thee any wager,
When we are both accoutred like young men,
I'll prove the prettier fellow of the two,
And wear my dagger with the braver grace,
And speak between the change of man and boy
With a reed voice, and turn two mincing steps
Into a manly stride, and speak of frays
Like a fine bragging youth, and tell quaint lies,
How honourable ladies sought my love,
Which I denying, they fell sick and died;
I could not do withal; then I'll repent,
And wish for all that, that I had not killed them;
And twenty of these puny lies I'll tell,
That men shall swear I have discontinued school
Above a twelvemonth. I have within my mind
A thousand raw tricks of these bragging Jacks,
Which I will practise.
NERISSA
Why, shall we turn to men?
PORTIA
Fie, what a question's that,
If thou wert near a lewd interpreter!
But come, I'll tell thee all my whole device
When I am in my coach, which stays for us
At the park gate; and therefore haste away,
For we must measure twenty miles to-day.

a) How is the theme of appearance & reality presented in this extract

b) How is the theme of appearance & reality presented in the play as whole?

☑ Make the point that appearance and reality is used for comedy and as a plot device

The theme of appearance and reality weaves its way throughout the play as Shakespeare shows us that what things seem like on the surface are often not what they really are. In the extract, Portia tells Nerissa her plan to disguise themselves as men to help Antonio and that **'when we are both accoutred like young men/ I'll prove the prettier fellow of the two'**. Her teasing comment reminds us how disguise is used to visually and humorously reflect the theme of appearance and reality. In Shakespeare's original productions, the character of Portia would have been played by a boy as women were forbidden by law to be actors. The audience would have been much entertained by the comedy of the boy actor pretending to be a girl who is pretending to be a boy. The comic element of the disguise is evident in Act 4 when, masquerading as the lawyer, Portia ironically responds to Bassanio's declaration that he would rather Portia were dead if it helped Antonio, saying **'your wife would give you little thanks for that, If she were by, to hear you make the offer'**. There is real humour here through **_dramatic irony_** as the audience is in on the joke; they know what Bassanio doesn't and can see the concealed Portia's indignation. Shakespeare often used disguise in his plays, drawing on the literary tradition of Greek and Roman theatre to engage the audience. Portia's decision to impersonate a man also acts as a **_plot device_**, increasing **_dramatic tension_** as she travels to Venice to save doomed Antonio. At this point in the play, the audience knows how determined Shylock is to have Antonio's **'pound of flesh'** and it is Portia that seems to be his only hope. We understand that her disguise will help move the plot along but she is mysterious and withholds the information, saying **'I'll tell thee all my whole device/ When I am in my coach'.** The veil of secrecy is intriguing and helps to keep the audience engaged as we wonder how her **'device'** will unfold.

✓ Make the point that the characters understand that appearance and reality are sometimes opposed

Portia mocks the manners of young men as she aspires to be **'like a fine bragging youth, and tell quaint lies, How honourable ladies sought my love'.** She is fully aware that young men lie and boast to present a more attractive version of themselves. Her father was also aware of this and so devised the casket task to protect Portia from deceptive men who would trick her into an unhappy marriage. The task fulfils its purpose as Bassanio rejects the gold casket, declaring **'thou gaudy gold/Hard food for Midas, I will none of thee'.** He understands that gold can dazzle and blind, and the hard *alliteration* of **'gaudy gold'** shows his contempt for the showy, flashy metal. He chooses the lead casket instead, fully understanding that appearances can be deceptive. His classical reference to the Greek myth of King Midas, whose touch turned everything to gold, reminds the audience that he is an educated man from a high-born family and so worthy of the lively, intelligent Portia.

✓ Move to the point that appearance and reality has a darker side

Yet although Portia talks humorously of how she will hide her female appearance and copy the manners of young men, there is perhaps a bitter side to her words and to her disguise. All of her life, Portia has been subject to the will of men and, in the extract, she seizes on the chance to play a man with all the power that she is normally denied. At the beginning of the play, she is forced to be passive as the foolish, arrogant suitors try their luck, being meek and polite to their faces but being fully aware of the men's faults. She has had the chance to observe the **'thousand raw tricks of these bragging Jacks'** and can now copy these as she pretends to be a man. There is perhaps frustrated contempt in her words with the *adjective* **'raw'** which suggests how unpolished and obvious young men are and a world-weary cynicism in the *hyperbolic* **'thousand'** that captures the extensive experience she has had of ambitious, arrogant men. She states that she will **'wear my dagger'** and while this is a lewd allusion to a penis to amuse the audience, the dagger does *symbolise* the power that Portia will have when she presents herself to society as a man. It is only through deceit and artifice that women can exert any power and break free from patriarchal control and Portia knows this and is perhaps angry about it. Elsewhere in the play, the theme also has a darker edge. In Act One, Antonio sneers at Shylock, saying that anyone can twist the truth to suit them: **'the devil can cite Scripture for his purpose'.** His *analogy* shows how he despises Shylock and sees him as evil, able to deceive at will. Yet even though Antonio does not trust Shylock who quotes from the Bible, he still does not see through Shylock's ruse and he signs the bond. Shylock manipulates Antonio by pretending to offer friendship, tricking Antonio and taking him to the brink of death. Shakespeare's audience would not have been familiar with Jews as Jews had been expelled from England in 1290. However, Christopher Marlowe's play, 'The Jew of Malta', performed in 1592 also portrays a money-obsessed, revenge-seeking Jew named Barabas; Shakespeare's portrayal of the mercenary Shylock is similar to Marlowe's and reinforced Elizabethan perceptions of Jews. Antonio's comparison of Shylock to the devil reflects these attitudes and reminds us of how reality can be masked for dark purposes.

✓ Finish by exploring whether the play values appearance over reality

Appearance is valued by all of the characters. All deceive each other and we see that any truthful reality does not actually bring happiness. For example, Jessica's last words of the play are **'I am never merry when I hear sweet music'**, suggesting that, far from being a joyous bride, she is already melancholy. The audience sees that the reality of marriage with Lorenzo, who took her away from her father hidden behind a mask, is not what she expected. Bassanio chooses the lead casket, not because he is Portia's true love, but because he himself deceives, borrowing money to give himself the impression of a rich suitor. His marriage is also based on a mirage. Yet this is only one interpretation and, by the end of the play, appearances have been stripped away. Bassanio admits to being a **'braggart'** and tells Portia the truth about the giving away of the ring. In turn, Portia reveals the truth about the doctor and 'his' clerk. Their marriage begins positively with mutual openness and honesty and, as the performance finishes, the audience is reassured that false appearances have all been stripped away.

The women in the play, Portia, Nerissa and Jessica, are all strong-minded, courageous characters. Shakespeare's portrayal of these characters encourages audiences to consider the role of women in the play and also within society.

> "her sunny locks/ Hang on her temples like a golden fleece"

- Bassanio describes Portia as a beautiful woman whose blonde hair resembles a golden fleece.

- The **simile** shows that Portia is being judged in terms of her appearance and her wealth. The golden fleece refers to the Greek myth in which Jason and his crew of Argonauts sailed in a quest which had the golden fleece as the prize.

Context: In the 16th century, marriages were often based at least in part on financial considerations. Women were expected to bring a dowry (sum of money) to their marriage. The way that Bassanio is interested in Portia as a prize suggests that he is motivated by her wealth rather than love.

> "so is the will of a living daughter curbed by the will of a dead father"

- Portia regrets that her father's casket task has left her unable to follow her own wishes and desires.

- The **parallel sentence structure** emphasises the binding power of her father's decision and how restricted Portia is.

- Portia's **pun** on 'will' reflects her wit and intelligence. Shakespeare presents her as a character to be admired.

Context: Wordplay or punning was popular with Elizabethan audiences and Shakespeare often uses it to entertain and to engage. Here, the pun on 'will' also reflects how Portia, as a woman in Renaissance Italy, has no independence and is controlled by the men in her life.

"superfluity comes sooner by white hairs, but competency lives longer"

• Nerissa gives Portia sensible advice, reminding her that excess living ages us and that to have just enough money means a longer, healthier life. Shakespeare uses Nerissa to remind the audience that desire for wealth can be damaging and so Nerissa is presented as wise and sensible.

• The warm, humorous friendship between the two women is fundamental in the play.

Context: Shakespeare's plays often celebrate the relationships between women, such as Hero and Beatrice in 'Much Ado About Nothing'.

"Our house is hell"

• Jessica decides to leave her unhappy household and marry Lorenzo.

• Her unhappiness is clearly shown through the *metaphor* comparing her home to hell. Rather than passively suffer, Jessica takes control of her own life and escapes with Lorenzo.

Context: In Venice, the Jewish community were forced to live by law in a segregated part of the city called a ghetto. Jessica's desire to leave her home and become Lorenzo's wife might well be founded in a desire for a better life rather than deep love for Lorenzo.

"I have within my mind/A thousand raw tricks of these bragging Jacks"

• Portia tells Nerissa her plan to disguise herself as a man to help Antonio. Portia humorously describes how she will copy the manners of men she has seen in order to be convincing in her disguise.

• She clearly mocks young men as **'bragging Jacks'**, poking fun at male bravado.

Context: In Shakespeare's original productions, the character of Portia would have been played by a boy as women were forbidden by law to be actors. The audience would have been much entertained by the comedy of the boy actor pretending to be a girl who is pretending to be a boy.

> "Tarry a little; there is something else. This bond doth give thee here no jot of blood"

- In the courtroom, Portia, masquerading as lawyer, uses the law to save Antonio from his grisly death. It is Portia, a woman, who is the hero of the play. Her intelligence and quick thinking stops Shylock from collecting the bond and killing Antonio. She is fully in control of the situation.

- The forceful **imperative verb** **'tarry'** (wait) shows that it is Portia in control in the courtroom, giving commands that the men have to abide by. The semi-colon creates a suspenseful pause after **'Tarry a little'**.

- Portia holds everyone's attention with her enigmatic **'there is something else'**, witholding the information and choosing when to deliver her stunning understanding of the law that will halt Shylock and save Antonio.

Grade 9 Exploration:
Look at the theme in a different way

Is 'The Merchant of Venice' a feminist text?

Yes: In the play, the women seem much more sensible and in control than their male counterparts. While Bassanio sighs over Antonio's fate with empty promises, Portia takes control of the situation, moving into a man's world to adeptly manipulate the male-dominated courtroom. Similarly, Jessica bravely risks everything for a better life while the sensible, humorous Nerissa compares favourably to her brash husband. The play certainly presents likeable, clever women who have influence and power.

No: Despite the audience's rapport with the female characters, they are not powerful figures. Any power that Portia does wield in the courtroom scene is because the other characters believe her to be a man; without her male disguise, she would be instantly silenced. She can only succeed in the male world if she denies or hides her femininity. Furthermore, the women are all subservient to the men. Portia gives herself entirely to Bassanio, saying, **'this house, these servants and this same myself/Are yours, my lord: I give them with this ring'**. The **list** emphasises that she is giving everything; interestingly, she places herself as the last item in the **list**, implying that the material possessions are of more interest. In the 16th century, women were the property of their husbands. They had no legal rights and could not own property; Portia's words may seem generous and selfless yet they also reflect the stark reality of the situation as she, and and all of her property and wealth, does indeed belong to Bassanio. Nerissa and Jessica are in similar positions and at the end, Jessica's last words are significant as she says **'I am never merry when I hear sweet music'**, suggesting that, far from being a joyous bride, she is already melancholy. Lorenzo's long speech encouraging her to enjoy the music could easily be interpreted as Lorenzo dominating and silencing his new wife.

The **_parallel sentence structure_** emphasises the binding power of Portia's father's decision and how restricted she is in making choices.

Rather than passively suffer, Jessica takes control of her own life and escapes with Lorenzo.

'so is the will of a living daughter curbed by the will of a dead father'

'Our house is hell'

Venice is a patriarchal society where women are restricted.

The women are strong characters.

Women

Male characteristics are mocked.

Is 'The Merchant of Venice' a feminist text?

'I have within my mind
A thousand raw tricks of these bragging Jacks'

Yes: The women seem much more sensible and in control than their male counterparts and it is witty, intelligent Portia who saves Antonio.

Portia pokes fun at male bravado. The audience would have been entertained by the comedy of the boy actor pretending to be a girl who is pretending to be a boy.

No: Despite the audience's rapport with the female characters, they are not powerful figures and are subservient to the men.

Read the following extract from Act 5 Scene 1.
Answer both questions below the text.
At this point in the play, Bassanio is in trouble with Portia for having given the ring away.

BASSANIO
Sweet Portia,
If you did know to whom I gave the ring,
If you did know for whom I gave the ring
And would conceive for what I gave the ring
And how unwillingly I left the ring,
When nought would be accepted but the ring,
You would abate the strength of your displeasure.
PORTIA
If you had known the virtue of the ring,
Or half her worthiness that gave the ring,
Or your own honour to contain the ring,
You would not then have parted with the ring.
What man is there so much unreasonable,
If you had pleased to have defended it
With any terms of zeal, wanted the modesty
To urge the thing held as a ceremony?
Nerissa teaches me what to believe:
I'll die for't but some woman had the ring.
BASSANIO
No, by my honour, madam, by my soul,

No woman had it, but a civil doctor,
Which did refuse three thousand ducats of me
And begg'd the ring; the which I did deny him
And suffer'd him to go displeased away;
Even he that did uphold the very life
Of my dear friend. What should I say, sweet lady?
I was enforced to send it after him;
I was beset with shame and courtesy;
My honour would not let ingratitude
So much besmear it. Pardon me, good lady;
For, by these blessed candles of the night,
Had you been there, I think you would have begg'd
The ring of me to give the worthy doctor.
PORTIA
Let not that doctor e'er come near my house:
Since he hath got the jewel that I loved,
And that which you did swear to keep for me,
I will become as liberal as you;
I'll not deny him anything I have,
No, not my body nor my husband's bed.

a) How are women and their position in society presented in the extract?

b) How are women and their position in society presented in the play as a whole?

 Start with the point that Portia is presented as a woman of great wit and intelligence

The three women in the play, Portia, Nerissa and Jessica, are all strong-minded, courageous characters. Shakespeare's portrayal of these characters encourage audiences to consider the role of women in the play and also within society. In this extract, Portia is presented as a quick-witted, clever woman as Bassanio tries to placate her with his reasons for giving the ring away and she immediately takes his words, twists them and uses them to her benefit. The ***repetitive sentence structure***, with each line ending with the expected words **'the ring'**, emphasises her quick-thinking intelligence and Bassanio, who thought to play down the situation, is very much on the backfoot. We see this humorous intelligence elsewhere in the play; in Act 1, Portia regrets that her father's casket task has left her unable to follow her own wishes and desires, saying **'so is the will**

of a living daughter curbed by the will of a dead father'. The *parallel sentence structure* emphasises the binding power of her father's decision and how restricted Portia is. Portia's **pun** on **'will'** (meaning both desire and a legal document) reflects her sharp wit as Shakespeare presents her as a character to be admired. Wordplay or **punning** was popular with Elizabethan audiences and Shakespeare often used it to entertain and to engage. Here, the **pun** on **'will'** also reflects how Portia, as a woman in Renaissance Italy, has no independence and is controlled by the men in her life despite her intelligence.

☑ Explore how much control the women have

To some extent, Portia retains control in this scene. Bassanio works very hard to try and win back Portia's favour, imploring **'what should I say, sweet lady?'** His *interrogative sentence structure* and the endearment **'sweet'** suggests that she is the dominant figure, yet this is not necessarily true. Bassanio is choosing to please her; he does not have to. In Act 3, Portia becomes subservient to her husband. She gives herself entirely to Bassanio, saying **'this house, these servants and this same myself/ Are yours, my lord: I give them with this ring'**. The **list** emphasises that she is giving everything; interestingly, she places herself as the last item in the **list**, implying that the material possessions are of more interest. In the 16th century, women were the property of their husbands. They had no legal rights and could not own property; Portia's words may seem generous and selfless yet they also reflect the stark reality of the situation as she, and and all of her property and wealth, does indeed belong to Bassanio. The same is true of Jessica and Nerissa, and, in Act Five, Jessica's last words are significant as she says **'I am never merry when I hear sweet music'**, suggesting that, far from being a joyous bride, she is already melancholy. Lorenzo's long speech encouraging her to enjoy the music could easily be interpreted as Lorenzo dominating and silencing his new wife. The women in the play do not have any real control against their husbands.

☑ Explore how far women are presented as superior to men

Despite their lack of power in a patriarchal society, the women seem much more sensible than their male counterparts and use their intelligence to take control when and where they can. While Bassanio sighs over Antonio's fate with empty promises, Portia takes charge of the situation, moving into a man's world to adeptly manipulate the male-dominated courtroom. In the extract, Bassanio refers to the doctor who saved Antonio as a **'worthy doctor'**. The *adjective* **'worthy'** reflects the respect that he feels for the clever 'man' who saved his friend at the last minute. Women were not allowed to practise law in Venice and so Portia has to disguise herself as a man in order to help Antonio. She masquerades as a lawyer to save Antonio from his grisly death, halting the moment of the cutting with **'tarry a little; there is something else. This bond doth give thee here no jot of blood'**. It is Portia, a woman, who is the hero of the play as her quick thinking stops Shylock from collecting the bond and killing Antonio. She is fully in control of the situation with the forceful *imperative verb* **'tarry'** (wait) showing that it is Portia in charge in the courtroom, giving commands that the men have to abide by. The semi-colon creates a suspenseful pause after **'tarry a little'** and Portia holds everyone's attention with her enigmatic **'there is something else'**, witholding the information and choosing when to deliver her stunning understanding of the law that will halt Shylock and save Antonio.

☑ Continue to explore how the women in the play are presented positively

The play certainly presents likeable, clever women who have integrity and good sense. Nerissa gives Portia sensible advice, reminding her that excess living ages us and that to have just enough money means a longer, healthier life: **'superfluity comes sooner by white hairs, but competency lives longer'**. Shakespeare uses Nerissa to remind the audience that desire for wealth can be damaging and Nerissa is shown to be wise and sensible. The warm, humorous friendship between the two women is fundamental in the play, and, indeed, Shakespeare's plays often celebrate the relationships between women, such as Hero and Beatrice in 'Much Ado About Nothing'. The other main female character is also a strong one; Jessica bravely risks everything for a better life, deciding to leave her unhappy household which is **'hell'** and marry Lorenzo. Her unhappiness is clearly shown through the *metaphor* comparing her home to hell and, rather than passively suffer, Jessica takes control of her own life and escapes with Lorenzo. Overall, the play is one with lively, strong women who we like and remember long after we have left the theatre.

14 Comedy
Exploration of a theme

'The Merchant of Venice' is a romantic comedy, a genre popular in Elizabethan theatre, with witty lovers who have to overcome barriers in order to be together. However, the play is sometimes defined as a tragicomedy due to the dark, painful moments.

"most vilely in the afternoon, when he is drunk"

- Portia states that she dislikes the Duke of Saxony's nephew when he is drunk.

- Portia's wit is established from the outset. She humorously refers to national stereotypes when she drolly *lists* her suitors and here refers to the contemporary perception that the Germans were heavy drinkers.

Context: Laughing at national stereotypes was acceptable in Elizabethan England and Portia's humorous dismissal of her multinational suitors would have been entertaining for Shakespeare's audience.

"Turn up on your right hand at the next turning, but, at the next turning of all, on your left"

- Launcelot confuses his father by sending him on a wild goose chase.

- There is visual, slapstick humour as the audience enjoys seeing the young man trick his bewildered father.

- The comedy here *juxtaposes* with the tension of the previous scene where the Prince of Morocco arrives in Belmont to take the casket test. Shakespeare deliberately delays the test, keeping the audience, and Portia, guessing about the outcome, by moving us from the suspense of the test straight into this comic scene of Lancelot teasing his father.

Context: Shakespeare drew on the Medieval tradition of jesters and fools by using clowns in his plays. These clowns entertained the groundlings (the commoners who only paid a penny to watch the play) but were also enjoyed by the nobility. Queen Elizabeth kept a fool at her court to amuse her.

"Three thousand ducats; well"

- Shylock muses on the amount of money that Antonio wishes to borrow.

- These are Shylock's first words of the play. Immediately, we associate Shylock with money and business. Shakespeare potentially creates the contemporary stereotype of the grasping, mercenary Jew, a farcial, comic figure for the audience to laugh at.

- The way he **repeats** the sum creates a sense of exagerrated greed around Shylock and the **interjection 'well'** suggests that he is musing on the prospect of making more money.

Context: Shakespeare's audience would not have been familiar with Jews as Jews had been expelled from England in 1290. However, Christopher Marlowe's play, 'The Jew of Malta', performed in 1592, just before 'The Merchant of Venice' was written, also portrays a money-obsessed, revenge-seeking Jew named Barabas; Shakespeare's portrayal of the mercenary Shylock is similar to Marlowe's and reinforced Elizabethan perceptions of Jews.

"Your wife would give you little thanks for that, If she were by, to hear you make the offer"

- Disguised as the lawyer, Portia ironically responds to Bassanio's declaration that he would rather Portia were dead if it helped Antonio.

- There is real humour here through **dramatic irony** as the audience is in on the joke; they know what Bassanio doesn't and can see the concealed Portia's indignation.

Context: Shakespeare often used disguise and mistaken identity in his plays, drawing on the literary tradition of Greek and Roman theatre to engage and entertain the audience.

"ring"

- The play ends with Portia teasing Bassanio over the ring that he gave away.

- The comedy lies in the lighthearted banter as Portia and Bassanio wage a war of words over the ring.

- There is also sexual innuendo attached to the rings. This bawdy humour appeals to Elizabethan and modern audiences.

Grade 9 Exploration:
Look at the theme in a different way

Is 'The Merchant of Venice' a straightforward romantic comedy?

Yes: Humour weaves its way throughout the play and is even used in the dramatic courtroom scene. The play ends with Bassanio begging Portia to **'forgive me this enforced wrong'** of the giving away of the ring. There is humour here for the audience as Portia teases him, and this humour wraps up the play which is, essentially, an engaging comedy.

Shakespeare follows the classic five act structure that was used in Greek theatre for romantic comedies. At the end of the play which marks the resolution of the conflict, all is forgiven and the characters are reconciled in a cheerful moonlit atmosphere of humour and harmony after the high drama of the courtroom.

No: There is too much pain at the end of the play to leave the audience satisfied that this is a straightforward comedy. Shylock loses everything: his wealth, his family, even his religion. At the end he is isolated, humiliated and silenced, and there is huge *pathos* (pity) as he utters his last words of the play: **'I pray you, give me leave to go from hence; I am not well'**. The audience sees him diminished and this leaves us uneasy. Similarly, there are tensions already present in the relationships. Love is seen as fickle as Gratiano states that he enjoys the thrill of the chase more than committed relationships, that women **'are with more spirit chased than enjoy'd'**; this does not bode well for his relationship with Nerissa. Furthermore, there are possible cracks in Jessica and Lorenzo's marriage already appearing; her last words of the play are **'I am never merry when I hear sweet music'** suggesting that, far from being a joyous bride, she is already melancholy. There is pain and tension woven into the lighthearted comedy.

There is real humour here through *dramatic irony* as the audience is in on the joke; they know what Bassanio doesn't and can see the concealed Portia's indignation.

Portia and Bassanio wage a light-hearted war of words over the ring. Their banter is heavy with sexual innuendo.

'Your wife would give you little thanks for that, If she were by, to hear you make the offer'

'ring'

Comedy is created through disguise and mistaken identity.

Humour is created through wordplay.

Comedy

The play uses comic characters.

Is 'The Merchant of Venice' a straightforward romantic comedy?

'Turn up on your right hand at the next turning, but, at the next turning of all, on your left'

Yes: Humour weaves its way throughout the play, ending with the cheerful resolution of the final scene.

Launcelot, the clown, confuses his father. Shakespeare drew on the Medieval tradition of jesters and fools by using clowns in his plays.

No: There is too much pain at the end for the play to be a straightforward comedy.

Read the following extract from Act 1 Scene 2.

Answer both questions below the text.

At this point in the play, Portia and Nerissa are discussing the casket task and Portia's suitors.

PORTIA
O me, the word 'choose!' I may
neither choose whom I would nor refuse whom I
dislike; so is the will of a living daughter curbed
by the will of a dead father. Is it not hard,
Nerissa, that I cannot choose one nor refuse none?
NERISSA
Your father was ever virtuous; and holy men at their
death have good inspirations: therefore the lottery,
that he hath devised in these three chests of gold,
silver and lead, whereof who chooses his meaning
chooses you, will, no doubt, never be chosen by
any rightly but one who shall rightly love. But what
warmth is there in your affection towards any of these
princely suitors that are already come?
PORTIA
I pray thee, over-name them; and as thou namest
them, I will describe them; and, according to my
description, level at my affection.

NERISSA
First, there is the Neapolitan prince.
PORTIA
Ay, that's a colt indeed, for he doth nothing but
talk of his horse; and he makes it a great
appropriation to his own good parts, that he can
shoe him himself. I am much afeard my lady his
mother played false with a smith.
NERISSA
Then there is the County Palatine.
PORTIA
He doth nothing but frown, as who should say 'If
you will not have me, choose:' he hears merry tales
and smiles not: I fear he will prove the weeping
philosopher when he grows old, being so full of
unmannerly sadness in his youth. I had rather be
married to a death's-head with a bone in his mouth
than to either of these. God defend me from these
two!

a) Write about how comedy is created in the extract.

b) Write about how comedy is created in the play as a whole.

☑ **Start with the point that 'The Merchant of Venice' is a romantic comedy**

'The Merchant of Venice' is a romantic comedy, a genre popular in Elizabethan theatre, with witty lovers who have to overcome barriers in order to be together. In this scene, we are introduced to Portia, the sharp, likeable heroine of the play who is frustrated because she is unable to find love on her own but is tied to her father's casket task. Yet even as she complains about her lack of choice, she does so with intelligent wit, stating that **'so is the will of a living daughter curbed by the will of a dead father.'** The ***parallel sentence structure*** emphasises the binding power of her father's decision and shows how restricted Portia is. Portia's ***pun*** on **'will'** reflects her wit and intelligence and so Shakespeare presents her as a character to be liked and admired. Wordplay or ***punning*** was popular with Elizabethan audiences and Shakespeare often uses it to entertain and to engage. Here, the ***pun*** on **'will'** also reflects how Portia, as a woman in Renaissance Italy, has no independence to exert her own will, and is controlled by the men in her life. Although she is being humourous, there is a world of impotent frustration caught up in her words. Portia's quick wit is evident throughout the play right until the end, where Portia teases Bassanio over the ring that he gave away. The comedy lies in the lighthearted banter as Portia and Bassanio wage a war of words over the ring. There is also sexual innuendo attached to the rings and this bawdy humour appeals to Elizabethan and modern audiences.

Move to the point that comedy is created through interaction between the characters

Portia and Nerissa's warm, close relationship allows the women to catalogue the suitors in a highly entertaining way. Nerissa sets up the comedy by introducing each hopeless suitor: **'first, there is the Neapolitan prince… Then there is the County Palatine'**. This enables Portia to describe her would-be husbands in an deliberately unflattering way. Later in the play, other interactions between characters also provide humour, for example, the comic scene of Lancelot tricking his father Gobbo by sending him on a wild goose chase. There is visual, slapstick humour as the audience enjoys seeing the young man trick his bewildered father. Shakespeare drew on the Medieval tradition of jesters and fools by using clowns in his plays. These clowns entertained the groundlings (the commoners who only paid a penny to watch the play) but were also enjoyed by the nobility such as Queen Elizabeth who kept a fool at her court to amuse her.

Make the point that comedy comes from stereotyping

Much of the humour of this extract comes from Portia's use of national stereotypes. She describes the Neapolitan prince as a **'colt'**, drawing on the perception that southern Italians were famous for their horsemanship, and ends her portrait of him with the lewd suggestion that **'I am much afeard my lady his mother played false with a smith'**. Her *hyperbolic* rejection of him and the County Palatine with the *exclamatory sentence* **'God defend me from these two!'** reflects her exaggerated disgust at the idea of marrying one of these stereotypes. Of course, this use of stereotypes prepares us for the central stereotype of the play with Shakespeare's depiction from the beginning of Shylock as a mercenary Jew. Shylock's first words of the play reflect this as he muses on the money that Antonio wishes to borrow, saying **'three thousand ducats; well.'** Immediately, we associate Shylock with money and business. Shakespeare potentially creates the contemporary stereotype of the grasping, mercenary Jew: a farcical, comic figure for the audience to laugh at. The way he *repeats* the sum creates a sense of greed around Shylock and the *interjection* **'well'** suggests that he is musing on the prospect of making more money. Shakespeare's audience would not have been familiar with Jews as Jews had been expelled from England in 1290. However, Christopher Marlowe's play, 'The Jew of Malta', performed in 1592, just before 'The Merchant of Venice' was written, also portrays a money-obsessed, revenge-seeking Jew named Barabas; Shakespeare's portrayal of the mercenary Shylock is similar to Marlowe's and reinforced Elizabethan perceptions of Jews. Early performances of Shylock often played to this stereotype in a comic way to amuse the audience although with changing attitudes over the years, this has given way to portrayals of Shylock as a victim, not as a figure of fun.

Continue to explore how far the play is a comedy

Humour weaves its way throughout the play and is even used in the dramatic courtroom scene. The play ends with Bassanio begging Portia to **'forgive me this enforced wrong'**. There is humour here for the audience, and this humour wraps up the play which is essentially an engaging comedy. Shakespeare follows the classic five act structure that was used in Greek theatre for romantic comedies. At the end of the play which marks the *resolution* of the conflict, all is forgiven and the characters are reconciled in a cheerful moonlit atmosphere of humour and harmony after the high drama of the courtroom. Yet surely there is too much pain at the end of the play to leave the audience satisfied that this is a straightforward comedy. Shylock loses everything: his wealth, his family, even his religion. At the end he is isolated, humiliated and silenced, and there is huge *pathos* (pity) as he utters his last words of the play: **'I pray you, give me leave to go from hence; I am not well'**. The audience sees him diminished and this leaves us uneasy. Similarly, there are tensions already present in the relationships. Love is seen as fickle as Gratiano states that he enjoys the thrill of the chase more than committed relationships, that women **'are with more spirit chased than enjoy'd'**; this does not bode well for his relationship with Nerissa. Furthermore, there are possible cracks in Jessica and Lorenzo's marriage already appearing; her last words of the play are **'I am never merry when I hear sweet music'** suggesting that, far from being a joyous bride, she is already melancholy. There is so much pain and tension woven into this comic play that many critics argue that it is a tragicomedy and certainly, while we laugh at the mistaken identity and the witty banter, we also uncomfortably watch the human suffering.

Quotations
Recap & Revise

Act 1 Scene 1

'In sooth, I know not why I am so sad'
Antonio is unsure why he feels unhappy.

'A stage where every man must play a part"
Antonio sees the world as 'a stage where every man must play a part'.

'dangerous rocks...enrobe the roaring waters with my silks'
Salerino refers to the perils of sea journeys.

'I owe the most in money and in love, And from your love I have a warranty'
Bassanio tells Antonio that he owes him a debt of money and friendship

'My purse, my person, my extremest means,/ Lie all unlock'd to your occasions'
Antonio promises his dear friend, Bassanio, to help him financially.

'her sunny locks
Hang on her temples like a golden fleece'
Bassanio describes Portia as a beautiful woman.

'all my fortunes are at sea'
Antonio admits that he has no spare money as he waits for his merchant ships to return to Venice.

Act 1 Scene 2

'so is the will of a living daughter curbed by the will of a dead father'
Portia regrets that her father's casket task prevents her following her own wishes.

'superfluity comes sooner by white hairs, but competency lives longer'
Nerissa gives Portia sensible advice, reminding her that excess living ages us.

'never be chosen by any rightly but one who shall rightly love'
Nerissa talks of how the casket task has been designed by Portia's father to ensure that only a man who truly loves her will be able to choose the right casket.

'most vilely in the afternoon, when he is drunk'
Portia states that she dislikes the Duke of Saxony's nephew when he is drunk.

Act 1 Scene 3

'Three thousand ducats; well'
Shylock muses on the amount of money that Antonio wishes to borrow.

'He lends out money gratis and brings down/ The rate of usance here with us in Venice'
Shylock hates Antonio because he lends money without interest.

'I hate him for he is a Christian'
Shylock states that he hates Antonio because of Antonio's religion.

'I will feed fat the ancient grudge I bear him'
Shylock clearly states that he plans revenge on Antonio.

'You call me misbeliever, cut-throat dog, And spit upon my Jewish gaberdine'
Shylock reminds Antonio about how he has been appallingly treated by him.

'The devil can cite Scripture for his purpose'
Antonio sneers at Shylock, saying that anyone can twist the truth to suit them.

'You shall not seal to such a bond for me: I'll rather dwell in my necessity'
Bassanio initially refuses to allow Antonio to accept Shylock's terms of the loan.

'I would be friends with you and have your love'
Shylock persuades Antonio to agree to his terms of the bond.

Act 2 Scene 2

'Turn up on your right hand at the next turning, but, at the next turning of all, on your left'
Launcelot confuses his father by sending him on a wild goose chase.

Act 2 Scene 2

'Our house is hell'
Jessica decides to leave her unhappy household and marry Lorenzo.

'But though I am a daughter to his blood, I am not to his manners'
Jessica says that she might have been born Jewish but her personality is different to her father's.

'O Lorenzo, if thou keep promise, I shall end this strife/ become a Christian and a loving wife'
Jessica decides to run away and marry Lorenzo.

Act 2 Scene 4

'gold and jewels she is furnish'd with'
Lorenzo states how Jessica will come to him with stolen valuables.

Act 2 Scene 5

'lock up my doors'
Shylock tells Jessica to keep the house safe.

Act 2 Scene 6

'are with more spirit chased than enjoy'd'
Gratiano states that he enjoys the thrill of the chase more than committed relationships.

'Lorenzo, certain, and my love indeed'.
Jessica checks that it is Lorenzo who is come, disguised in a mask, to take her from Shylock's house.

'gild myself/With some more ducats'
Jessica takes more money before leaving with Lorenzo.

'For she is wise, if I can judge of her'
Lorenzo praises Jessica's intelligence.

Act 3 Scene 4

'How true a gentleman'
Lorenzo speaks highly of Antonio.

Act 2 Scene 8

'My daughter! O my ducats! O my daughter! Fled with a Christian!'
Shylock is devastated when his daughter takes his money and runs away.

'I think he only loves the world for him'
Salanio says that Antonio has an incredibly deep love for Bassanio.

Act 3 Scene 1

'If you prick us, do we not bleed? If you tickle us, do we not laugh? If you poison us, do we not die?'
Shylock challenges the Venetians to see him as a human being.

'I thank thee, good Tubal: good news!'
Shylock is grateful to Tubal for news.

'Thou stickest a dagger in me'
Shylock finds Tubal's news distressing.

'A ring he had of your daughter for a monkey'
Tubal tells Shylock how Jessica is spending huge amounts of money, and how Jessica has sold her mother's ring.

Act 3 Scene 3

'I will have my bond'
Shylock is determined to have his bond.

Act 3 Scene 2

**'thou gaudy gold,
Hard food for Midas, I will none of thee'**
Bassanio rejects the gold casket.

'This house, these servants and this same myself/ Are yours, my lord: I give them with this ring'
Portia consents to marry Bassanio.

'confirm'd, sign'd, ratified by you'
Bassnio tells Portia that she needs to agree to their engagement.

'you shall see how much I was a braggart'
Bassanio admits that he was overconfident at the start of the play.

Act 4 Scene 1

'The duke cannot deny the course of the law'
Antonio states that Shylock is entitled to his gruesome bond by law and no one, not even the duke, can stop him.

'The Jew shall have my flesh, blood, bones and all'
Bassanio offers himself to save Antonio.

'The weakest kind of fruit drops earliest to the ground'
Antonio accepts his death, saying that he is weak and so will die young.

'Why dost thou whet thy knife so earnestly?'
Bassanio watches Shylock eagerly sharpening the knife to cut Antonio.

'abject and in slavish parts'
Shylock exposes the Christians' lack of mercy and compassion when he accuses them of treating their slaves in an inhumane way.

'Your wife would give you little thanks for that,/If she were by, to hear you make the offer'
Disguised as the lawyer, Portia responds to Bassanio's declaration that he would rather Portia were dead if it helped Antonio.

'Tarry a little; there is something else. This bond doth give thee here no jot of blood'
Portia stops Shylock from killing Antonio by using Venice's laws.

'The Jew shall have all justice'
Portia traps Shylock in the courtroom.

'Portia, forgive me this enforced wrong'
Bassanio begs Portia to forgive him for giving away the ring.

'it droppeth as the gentle rain from heaven'
Portia states the mercy comes from God.

'I pray you, give me leave to go from hence; I am not well'
Shylock leaves the courtroom as a broken man.

Act 5 Scene 1

'in such a night/ Troilus methinks mounted the Troyan walls'
Newly-weds Lorenzo and Jessica talk of the moonlit night, comparing it nights in which famous lovers met.

**'In such a night
Did pretty Jessica, like a little shrew,
Slander her love, and he forgave it her'**
Lorenzo banters with Jessica in the moonlit night at Belmont.

'I am never merry when I hear sweet music'
Jessica is melancholy at the end.

'If I could add a lie unto a fault, I would deny it'
Bassanio is forced to explain why he is not wearing Portia's ring.

Glossary
Explanation of terms

ADJECTIVE - a word that describes a noun e.g. 'dangerous rocks'

ADVERB - a word that describes a verb e.g. 'Why dost thou whet thy knife so earnestly?'

ALLITERATION - repetition of the same letter in words next to or near each other e.g. 'gaudy gold'

ANALOGY - comparison of one thing to another e.g. 'The devil can cite Scripture for his purpose'

CLAUSE - a group of words that contains a verb

CONDITIONAL TENSE - tense that speculates on what might or could happen e.g. 'but if you please'

CONJUNCTION - word that joins two clauses e.g. 'therefore' 'but' 'and' 'yet'

CONTRAST - when something is very different from something elsee'

DECLARATIVE SENTENCE - a sentence that states a fact e.g. 'I am arm'd and well prepared'

DRAMATIC IRONY - when the audience knows something the characters do not

EXCLAMATORY PHRASE OR SENTENCE - a sentence or phrase that shows excitement or emotion e.g. 'My daughter! My ducats!'

HYPERBOLE - exagerrated or dramatic language e.g. 'were in six parts and every part a ducat'

IMAGE - powerful words or phrase that paints a picture in our heads

IMPERATIVE VERBS - verbs that give orders e.g. 'Give me your hand, Bassanio'

INTERJECTION - word or words that are added to a main clause and often express an emotion e.g. 'Three thousand ducats: well'

INTERROGATIVE SENTENCE STRUCTURE - sentences that ask questions e.g. 'How shalt thou hope for mercy, rendering none?'

JUXTAPOSITION- two themes or ideas or atmospheres placed next to each other or contrasting effect

LIST - a group of ordered items or actions e.g. 'this house, these servants and this same myself'

METAPHOR - desciding a person or object as something else e.g. 'enrobe the roaring waters with my silks'

MINOR SENTENCE - an incomplete sentence e.g. 'My daughter!'

MODAL VERBS- verbs that show a level of certainty e.g. 'The duke cannot deny the course of the law'

NOUN - name of an object/place/time/emotion

PARALLEL SENTENCE STRUCTURE - a balance within one or more sentences of similar phrases or clauses that have the same grammatical structure e.g. 'so is the will of a living daughter curbed by the will of a dead father'

PATHOS - sadness

PLOT DEVICE - technique used to move narrative along

POSSESSIVE PRONOUN - a pronoun that shows ownership e.g. 'My purse'

PRONOUN - a word that replaces a proper noun e.g. 'one half of me is yours'

PUN - wordplay or jokes on words that have more than one meaning e.g. 'so is the will of a living daughter curbed by the will of a dead father'

RHETORICAL QUESTION - question that does not need an answer e.g. 'If you prick us, do we not bleed?'

REPETITION - when a word or phrase is repeated e.g. 'one half of me is yours, the other half yours... so all yours'

SETTING - where a scene is played out e.g. the setting of Act Five is the moonlit garden on Belmont

SIMILE - describing a person or object as something else using 'like' or 'as' e.g. 'her sunny locks/ Hang on her temples like a golden fleece'

STRUCTURE - the order in which events happen in a story

SYNTAX - order of words in a sentence

TONE - mood or atmosphere

VERB - an action word

Milton Keynes UK
Ingram Content Group UK Ltd.
UKHW050938100923
428409UK00002B/9

9 781916 382701